3.03

Give Peace a Chance

JOHN FERGUSON

Gooday Publishers

FOR MARY MARTIN

First Published in 1988 by Gooday Publishers
P.O. Box 60, East Wittering, West Sussex PO20 8RA

© John Ferguson 1988

British Library Cataloguing in Publication Data

Ferguson, John, 1921 –
  Give peace a chance.
  1. Social Protest – Non-violent action
  I. Title
  322.4'4

ISBN 1 – 870568 – 07 – 9

Typeset in Plantin by Woodfield Graphics, Fontwell, West Sussex.
Printed in Great Britain by Hollen Street Press, Slough, Berks.

Contents

Foreword

The episodes recorded below all exemplify nonviolent action. This may take various forms, but fundamentally they all refuse to meet violence (whether war, military aggression, oppression or personal assault) with counter-violence, but seek instead a positive and constructive action which may transform the situation. This almost always involves a willingness to suffer violence or death rather than inflict it. This may arise from a religious commitment, such as that of the early Christians, and many later Christians, Quakers, Mennonites, Brethren and others from every branch of the Church, in obedience to the command 'Love your enemies' and their understanding of the cross as God's way of changing the world. Buddhists and Jains, again, have stood by 'reverence for life' and Buddhists in particular have stressed the action springing from compassion. Or it may arise from a humanist and humanitarian sense that good will not come out of evil; that to respond to violence with violence is to be dragged down to the level of the original user; that recourse to violence undermines the very values it is designed to protect. Or it may arise from a cool calculation that violence tends to escalate, and that if one side refuses violence, the sum of violence is more than halved. The sociologist P. A. Sorokin, who once said "The whole of sociology can be summed up in six words, 'Love breeds love; hate breeds hate'," showed by experiments with young disturbed adults that a firm, constructive, loving response stands a 19 to 1 chance of meeting their violence successfully as compared with a violent or repressive discipline.

A. Ruth Fry's Victories without Violence has been a precious and inspiring book for many of us. It has needed redoing for this generation, partly because its style is somewhat old-fashioned, partly because there are many recent or recently discovered examples of nonviolent action to inspire others. Ruth Fry stressed individual action. I do not believe that she was wrong in this; we need our heroes still, our models and exemplars. But we need also to remember Brecht's words that it was not the Pharaohs who built the pyramids, but unnamed ordinary people. Further unless the corporate quality of nonviolent action can be seen it will not induce allegiance. So I have tried to combine records of leadership and of communal action.

The core of the collection remains Christian action. I have singled out a few examples from other traditions, and brought the early ones together under the heading 'Pre-Christian' even though two fall into the Christian era; I have also kept a special awareness of twentieth-century actions from India and further East, and for developments within the United Nations.

Lesley Roff has given the book a flying start by her typing: many thanks.

John Ferguson

PART I: PRE-CHRISTIAN

1 Elisha and the Aramaeans

The Hebrew prophet Elisha was not always a man of compassion. But there is one notable story about him. The Aramaeans were trying to capture him. Elisha prayed, saying to his trembling servant "Do not be afraid, for those who are with us are more than those who are with them." He was speaking of spiritual powers. The Aramaeans were deluded, and found themselves in the city of Samaria, surrounded by the Israelite army. The King of Israel said excitedly "My father, shall I smite them? Shall I smite them?" But Elisha told him to let them eat and drink and return to their master. And Aramaean raids on Israel ceased.

Source: 2 Kings 6,8 – 23

2 The First Good Samaritan

The northern kingdom of Israel had committed an act of aggression against the southern kingdom of Judah, and taken a large number of prisoners. A Samaritan prophet named Oded went out to meet the army and insisted on the return of the prisoners of war. "They clothed them, gave them sandals, provided them with food and drink, and anointed them; and carrying all those who were tottering from exhaustion on the back of asses they brought them to their kinsfolk at Jericho, the city of palm trees."

Did Jesus have this story in mind when he was asked what love of neighbour means?

Source: 2 Chronicles 28,1 – 15.

3 The Suffering Servant

In the book named after Isaiah there are four songs which speak of the Servant of God. The songs are fluid; sometimes God speaks and the Servant is "he". Sometimes the Servant is speaking and God is "he". At one point the Servant is Israel, at another he is an individual called to bring Israel to God. To some the fourth song is a vision, to others it is a vividly historical account of one who has died: "He was wounded for our transgressions, he was bruised for our iniquities: upon him was the chastisement that made us whole, and with his stripes we are healed."

There is only one person who can lead Israel, be representative of Israel, and be called Israel, and that is the King. Jehoiachin gave himself up to save Jerusalem from being utterly sacked. We do not know anything for certain about his death, but we do know that he was released by Evil-Merodach and treated with remarkable honour, and it is at least plausible that he was released and fêted in order to be put to death as a royal substitute the following year.

Behind the songs are four thoughts about suffering. First, suffering is the natural consequence of sin. Second, in a world in which suffering exists as the penalty for doing wrong, the innocent are called by God to offer their willingness to suffer in order to bring others back to him. Third, this is the way of redemption both corporate and individual; the Jewish scriptures know nothing of one morality for the individual and another for the nation. Fourth, there is a fulfilment both on earth and beyond death. The Servant, because he has died, will see the fruit of the travail of his soul and be satisfied. The fruit is the practical result on earth, but his discernment of this lies beyond the grave. And the Jews did return from exile.

Not all scholars will accept the reference to Jehoiachin: at least he is one who suffered for his people.

Sources: 2 Kings 24,12; 25,27 – 30;
Isaiah 42,1 – 4; 49,1 – 6; 50,4 – 9; 52,13 – 53,12

4 The Jains

There is no dramatic story to tell of Mahavira, the founder of the Jains. He lived at about the same time as the Buddha. He is the great apostle of *ahimsa*, non-harming. "One may not kill, ill-use, insult, torment, or persecute any kind of living being, any kind of creature, any kind of thing having a soul, any kind of being. That is the pure, eternal, enduring commandment of religion which has been proclaimed by the sages who comprehend the world."

So the Jains gave up hunting; they abandoned meat-sacrifice; they became vegetarians. They even gave up agriculture, since it seemed impossible to dig the soil without damage to the minute living organisms which inhabit it. The Jain monk will not light a fire or lamp, for fear of destroying insects, and because of respect for the living fire itself. He fixes his eyes on the ground to avoid treading on an insect, and filters his breath through a veil to avoid damage to the insects in the air.

These negative precepts arise from reverence for life and compassion.

Sources: D. Bhargava *Jaina Ethics*;
S. Stevenson *The Heart of Jainism*

5 The Buddha
(c. 560 – 480 BC)

Siddharta Gautama was born a prince. According to one story a seer said that he was destined to be a world-ruler, or, if he should set eyes in succession upon a man decrepit with age, a man afflicted by plague, a dead body and a monk, he would be a homeless wanderer. His father tried to shield him from these portents. In vain. Aware of decay, disease and death, he renounced power and privilege, and went in search of enlightenment. In meditation under the bo-tree (*ficus religiosa*) Truth came: Life is suffering; to extinguish suffering we must extinguish desire or attachment to the world. He was now the Buddha, the Enlightened One.

There are few moments of high drama in the Buddha's life, but this was one. He could at that moment have entered absolute Nirvana, the heaven-haven which is the annihilation of desire, and liberation from the world. This was a temptation to be overcome. He looked with compassion upon suffering mankind. He was the lotus who had emerged from the waters and flowered; he must still help other buds to open to the sun.

So for forty-five years he wandered as a homeless preacher, proclaiming the Four Noble Truths, that all life is suffering, that suffering comes from desire, that suffering can be destroyed if desire is extirpated, and that the way to this is an Eightfold Path.

The Eightfold Path involves Right Action, and that includes the refusal to kill, and the practice of a love which does no harm to any. It also involves Right Vocation, the refusal to follow a profession harmful to others, such as the arms trade or a military career. The basic rules of social behaviour as expressed in *The Dhammapada* are:

Anger must be overcome by the absence of anger;
Evil must be overcome by good;
Greed must be overcome by liberality;
Lies must be overcome by truth.

6

The Buddha is quoted as saying, "Everyone is afraid of violence; everyone likes life. If one compares oneself with others, one would never take life or be involved in the taking of life."

One characteristic story of the Buddha is called the Sermon on Abuse. A fellow came up and shouted abuse at him. The Buddha said, "If someone offered me a gift and I returned it, whose would it be?" "The original owner's." "Just so. I do not accept your abuse. I return it to you." He went on "If someone spits at the sky the spittle soils, not the sky but his own face. If someone throws dust into the wind it blows back on to him." According to the story the Buddha's refusal to be provoked, his gentle firmness and his wise words converted the abuser.

Sources: *The Dhammapada*; *The Life of the Buddha*.

6   Asoka Maurya
(3rd Century BC)

Asoka's grandfather, Chandragupta, was a soldier and an empire-builder. Asoka became ruler of the Magadhan empire in north India about the year 270 BC, and continued a career of imperialistic conquest.

Then, about nine years after his accession, he was converted to the Buddhist way of life or *dhamma*, and became a lay adherent of the Buddha's teaching.

It is hard to say whether revulsion from war led the emperor towards enlightenment, or whether his acceptance of the eight-fold path led him to revulsion from war, or whether, somehow, the two happened together. However it was, Asoka turned from war to peace. He called his subjects and neighbouring states alike to accept the greatest of gifts, brotherly kindness to all living beings, truth, justice, patience, understanding, and an active aspiration to higher things.

Over his kingdom he erected pillars bearing the new edicts. One of them shows the transformation in him:

> The Beloved of the Gods. The Compassionate King in the ninth year of his reign conquered the Kalingas. One hundred and fifty thousand persons were thence carried away captive, one hundred thousand were there slain, and many times that number perished.

> Ever since the annexation of the Kalingas, the Beloved of the Gods has zealously protected the *dhamma*, has been devoted to that law and has proclaimed its precepts.

> The Beloved of the Gods feels remorse on account of the conquest of the Kalingas, because during the subjugation of a previously unconquered country, slaughter, death and the taking away captive of the people necessarily occur, whereat The Beloved of the Gods feels profound sorrow and regret...

> The only true conquest is that effected through the *dhamma*, which avails both for this world and the next. Let all the pleasures of

my sons be the pleasure of exertion which avails both for this world
and the next.

In another edict he says, "Whatever exertion I make, I strive
only to discharge the debt I owe to all living beings." This is
a radically new concept of government.

So Asoka became a man of peace. From the conquest of the
Kalingas, there are no records of war during his reign. Even the
wild tribes of forest and mountain were not repressed by force
of arms, but called to share in the new way of life.

Peace to Asoka was not just refraining from violence. It
involved positive steps to look after the well-being of his people,
even in their physical needs. So he built hospitals. He improved
the water supply and the conservation of water. Alongside this,
he built *stupas* in honour of the Buddha. In this he fostered one
of the most glorious periods of Indian art. His edicts proclaim
him "The Compassionate One".

Asoka was a missionary for his religion, and he sent mes-
sengers to proclaim the way of truth through India and beyond.
His emissaries went to Syria, Egypt, Cyrene, Macedonia, Epirus,
and, closer at hand, to Sri Lanka.

For thirty years he ruled in peace and wisdom. India was no
doubt a dictatorship, but it was certainly a benevolent dictatorship, paternalistic but constructive. Christmas Humphreys wrote
of him, "His power was absolute and exercised, it seems, entirely
for good...by his kindliness to all men and to all living things, his
tolerance for all points of view, and his powerful exhortations to
all men to live the Buddha-life, he set an example which few, if
any, of the rulers of history have even attempted to attain."

Source: V.A. Smith *Asoka*

7   The Followers of Tao (6th – 5th centuries)

The *Tao Te Ching*, the Way-Power-Book, is one of the great treatises of religious mysticism and religious pacifism. It is attributed to a shadowy figure named Lao-Tzu, whom K'ung (Confucius) called a dragon.

The right life is one in harmony with the Tao, the ultimate Way. To find and follow the Tao involves *wu-wei*, non-effort, not striving, receptivity. The image of water is used; it benefits all things without striving and settles naturally in the lowest place.

The direction of the book is clear. Militarism comes from striving. The less government, the better. Weapons are instruments of evil. Only when a people have fallen away from the Tao are war horses found on the frontiers; when Tao prevails, the horses are dunging the fields. Violence escalates, and war brings famine. To yield is to be preserved whole; to be bent is to become straight. When two armies face one another, victory lies with the one that yields. Peace is the natural state of mankind.

The result was a strong movement of peace-makers recorded in the *Chuang-Tzu*:

> They sought to unite men through an ardent love in universal brotherhood. To fight against lusts and evil desire was their chief endeavour. When they were reviled, they did not consider it a shame; they were intent on nothing but the redemption of men from quarrelling. They forbade aggression, and preached disarmament in order to redeem mankind from war. This teaching they carried throughout the world. They admonished princes and instructed subjects. The world was not ready to accept their teaching, but they held to it all the more firmly. It was said that high and low tried to avoid meeting them, but that they forced themselves on people.

Sources: *Tao Te Ching*; *Chuang-Tzu*

10

8 Chang Lu (c. AD 200)

Later followers of the Tao fell away from its high standards, and degenerated into superstition and magic. Not all. Chang Lu founded a small Taoist state in the upper valley of the Han between Shensi and Szuchuan. The administrators were all committed Taoists, and they tried to live out their faith in their politics. The citizens were invited to a regular process of self-examination. The government was not eager to intervene even when offences took place, and it was a general rule that offenders were not punished until they had offended three times. Further the basic punishment for anti-social action repeated in this way, was social service in the form of road-mending. One innovation was the introduction of hostelries in which travellers could receive bed and board free, and the availability of food outside these hostelries for any in need. The whole régime was marked by integrity, mildness and tolerance. It flourished from about AD 188–215.

Source: R. C. Zaehner (ed.)
The Concise Encyclopaedia of Living Faiths

9 Ancient Rome

Political life at Rome was controlled by a relatively small number of aristocratic families. The commons had no say in government. They were excluded from religious and political office, and from intermarriage with the nobles. There was in the early Republic no codification of the law, and people were subject to arbitrary action. There was land hunger and pressure of debt.

What defence had the powerless against the all-powerful nobles? They could have risen violently and assassinated the consuls, the supreme officers of state. They did not do so. They used *secession* or withdrawal, a form of general strike, withdrawing *en masse* outside the city boundaries, to the nearby Aventine hill or some other point or refuge. This was a voluntary emigration and abstention from public life. A community cannot do without its men in the street, and the action was an effective form of pressure on those in power, without recourse to violence. The struggle for power went on for over two centuries, during which five 'secessions' are recorded. We cannot be certain of the historicity of all of them, but the last one, in 287 BC, was certainly historical, and equally certainly was not the first. By tradition, the commons succeeded in achieving the restoration of constitutional government which had been suspended, the codification of law, the appointment of their own officers or tribunes with personal sacrosanctity and a right of veto, rights of intermarriage, and eventually the right to pass legislation called *plebiscita*, which had binding power on all citizens.

It will not do to overstate what the commons achieved. Power remained in practice largely with the aristocrats. But the people now had rights and protection. There had been civil war for two centuries, but it had been, in modern parlance, a cold war. A hundred and fifty years after the commons achieved their aims civil disputes broke out into violence, and Rome had a century of appalling civil war. It is to the credit of the *plebs* that their revolution was nonviolent.

Sources: Livy, Dionysius of Halicarnassus, Diodorus Siculus

10 Diogenes (4th century BC)

The word 'Cynic' has changed its name. It really means 'Dogged' or 'Dog-like'. The first Cynics practised 'non- attachment'. They were extreme individualists. Like pariah dogs they owned no master, and felt no shame. They renounced citizenship, possessions, everything. Their famous founder, Diogenes, used a huge wine-jar for shelter, and only a scrip, and in old age, a staff besides. Asked 'Nationality?' the Cynic replied 'I am a citizen of the universe.' To a Cynic, war was abject folly. In one of the best anecdotes of antiquity, the news reaches Corinth that Philip of Macedon is on the march. Immediately there is a regular to-do. One man is polishing his armour, another is wheeling stones, another patching the wall. In the midst, Diogenes is sitting unconcerned. Then suddenly he rises and rolls his jar with vigour along the street, and then rolls it back again, for he too must join in the general business. It would be difficult to devise a more biting comment on the futility of war.

Source: Diogenes Laertius

11 The Epicureans

There are no dramatic stories of peace-making to tell of the Epicureans. The very name has come to be maligned—to the Jews an atheist, to later Europe a pleasure-seeker. Yet Epicurus, who lived at Athens round about the year 300 BC, believed in gods, though not in gods concerned with human life, and in seeking happiness, argued pessimistically for the course of action in which the excess of pain over pleasure would be minimized. This was never war. The Roman Epicurean poet Lucretius began his great poetic account of the philosophy with the ancient myth of how Venus (in his poem, Peace) persuades Mars (War) to lay aside his weapons.

The Epicureans were politically quietist. It was said of them, by contrast with the Stoics, that they would not enter public life unless forced. Epicurus had a house with a garden between Athens and the sea. In that garden the fellowship met, living simply, with no barriers—men and women, children and adults, slaves and free men, Greeks and foreigners, all were welcome. Epicurus believed in friendship; he once said, 'Friendship dances round the world, calling all mankind to awaken to the praises of a life of happiness.'

Centuries later, an Epicurean named Diogenes—not to be confused with Diogenes the Dog—had placed round the city-centre of Oenoanda in Asia Minor, in letters carved in stone, the gospel of Epicurus, which he calls 'the prescription of salvation'. He says that he does so not least for the sake of those who are wrongly called foreigners. There is in reality only one country, the earth, and one nation, the human race.

Sources: Epicurus, Lucretius, Diogenes of Oenoanda

12 Musonius Rufus (1st century AD)

Musonius Rufus was a Stoic with Cynic leanings, something of a saint and something of a radical. The Stoics were believers in the brotherhood of all mankind. The Cynics were individualistic practitioners of non-attachment who saw patriotism, partisanship and war-making (whether defensive or offensive) as futile. AD 69 was a year of terrible civil war for the Romans: it has been called 'the year of the four emperors'. But the Romans were militarist. Our word 'virtue' is derived from the Latin *virtus*, courage in battle. As the armies confronted one another in a temporary truce, Musonius 'began to go round the soldiers, expatiating on the benefits of peace and the risks of war'. *Romana virtus* prevailed. The habits of war were too deeply ingrained. He was met with jeers, yawns, warnings and threats of violence. Yet, though he failed to prevent renewed bloodshed, his was a real ministry of reconciliation, and he showed a truer courage, a juster sense of what it means to be a man, than those who reviled him.

Source: Tacitus; M. P. Charlesworth, *Five Men*

PART II: JESUS

13 Jesus

The Jewish people had an apocalyptic dream in which the Messiah, the Anointed, was to be the deliverer, the liberator from foreign rule, and there was a strong tradition that he would be a military conqueror entering his city high upon a white charger to lead a liberation movement and throw whatever power was oppressing the Jews into the sea, and proclaim a kingdom of peace and justice.

When Jesus set out upon his public ministry he faced this temptation, for the temptation to secure the kingdoms of the world on terms not God's (and the record of the temptation can only have come from him) must have been this. Instead he proclaimed love towards enemies, including the hated Romans.

Some followed him in the hope of such an uprising—Simon the Zealot almost certainly, possibly Simon Peter Bariona (an Aramaic nickname for a guerrilla: it was Simon who tried to defend Jesus by the sword, and was rebuked), possibly Judas Iscariot (?*sicarius*; was the 'betrayal' an attempt to force Jesus into military revolt), possibly James and John ('the sons of thunder,' who wanted to call down fire from heaven on an unsympathetic village). After his death two disciples leaving Jerusalem for Emmaus were regretfully reflecting that they had hoped he might be the liberator. But, though Jesus welcomed these men, he welcomed also Matthew the tax-gatherer or collaborator, whom most Zealots would gladly have assassinated. He healed the batman of a Roman centurion, whom most Zealots would have been happy to see dead.

We can point to three key-moments in the ministry of Jesus. One is the only miracle-story to appear in all four gospels. We call it the Feeding of the Five Thousand. The people flock to him. He tries to escape from them across the lake, but they follow him round the shore. He has pity on them, for they are as sheep without a shepherd; we happen to know that the phrase was used in the military resistance, of those looking for a leader. He taught them. What? It cannot have been anything very different from the Sermon on the Mount—the all-embracing love of enemies. He then organized them into military companies, by fifties and hundreds, and shared a meal with them and sent them away. He was indeed the Messiah, but not the sort they expected. John, the most politically alert of the gospel-writers, tells us that at this time they tried to crown him king, but he would not have it.

The second key-moment is at Caesarea Philippi. He asks the disciples who people think he is. The reply comes back: Elijah, or John the Baptist or some other prophet. What do the disciples think? Peter blurts out 'You're the Messiah.' Jesus's tone is teasing. 'Blessed are you, Simon Bariona'—Simon the Revolutionary—'that was inspiration.' Then he goes on to tell that the Son of Man must suffer, and when Peter protests, calls him 'Satan'. Peter is renewing the earlier temptation.

The third key-moment is at his entry to Jerusalem. He chooses to enter, not on a white charger, but on a donkey. This fulfilled a vision of Zechariah, of the king who enters to bring not military revolt and war, but disarmament and peace. As he looks on the city, Jesus cries unashamedly. He is laying before his people a choice—nonviolent suffering love, or violent uprising. His way is the first, but he knows theirs would be the second, and he knows the dreadful requital that would follow.

So he goes to the Cross, as he has foretold he would. He is no political quietist. Crucifixion was the Roman penalty for revolutionary activity. He is the true revolutionary, the non-violent revolutionary. In the garden at his arrest he rebukes the follower who tries to defend him with the sword: 'Put up your sword into its place. All those who take the sword shall perish by the sword.' In those words, said Tertullian, he disarms every soldier. He rebukes, not offensive violence, but defensive violence, all violence for however good a cause and blameless and selfless a motive. The choice 'Barabbas or Jesus,' is again the moment of truth, for 'Barabbas was a robber'—that is a guerrilla, a freedom-fighter. It is the choice of violent uprising against an unjust régime, and a commitment to nonviolence and a willingness to suffer.

19

But the death of Jesus was not a defeat for nonviolent love. It has ever since been seen as a victory. Jesus lived on, lived on in the lives of those who accepted him, lives on still. This is true whatever view one takes of the Resurrection. He conquered Rome from inside not outside.

Source: *The New Testament*

PART III: MAINLY PERSONAL

14 Vibia Perpetua

Vibia Perpetua was twenty-two, a young woman from Carthage, belonging to the upper classes. To the great distress of her family, she became a Christian, and, in a time of persecution, was arrested. With her was her maid, a slave named Felicitas. There were men arrested too, but it is Perpetua and Felicitas, mistress and maid, freewoman and slave, whom we remember above all.

Perpetua had a dream. She saw a golden ladder reaching to the sky, and underneath a dragon. One of the men, Saturus, set foot on the ladder and told her to follow. She named Jesus, trod on the dragon's head and climbed. She reached a garden and found an old shepherd milking his flock. He welcomed her and gave her cheese to eat. As she ate it she heard a vast crowd shout "Amen!" She awoke, and knew that the outcome would be martyrdom, and that Saturus would go first.

In the arena they faced wild animals. As their blood flowed the crowd cried in imitation of the baptismal cry "Washed and saved!" A soldier asked Saturus for his ring. The Christian gave it saying "Remember my faith." The bear detailed to crush him refused to touch him. Perpetua and Felicitas were stripped and immobilized in a net to be gored by a wild cow. Perpetua was in a state of ecstasy and felt no pain. They were finished off with the sword, Saturus first, as in the dream. Perpetua cried out when her breast was pierced, then firmly guided the sword to her throat, "and possibly" (the account goes on) "such a woman could not have been slain unless she had willed it herself, since the impure spirit was afraid of her."

Tertullian, himself a convert perhaps through seeing the bearing of Christians under martyrdom, who may (by then a Christian himself) having watched these very sights, said "The blood of Christians is seed." For a martyr means a witness, and the courage of these women under cruelty led many to seek the source of such courage.

Source: *Acts of Perpetua*

15 How the Gladiatorial Games were Ended

One of the darkest stains on the story of ancient Rome was the gladiatorial fights—the "games" as they were called—men butchering one another for the sadistic sport of the spectators. Some people with a sense of humanity protested; when it was proposed to introduce the games into Athens, one philosopher said "First destroy the Altar of Pity"; but they went on. When the Roman Empire became Christian, they still went on.

So the scene is Christian Rome; the date about AD 400; the place that gigantic amphitheatre we call the Colosseum. It is the day of the games. The great silk awnings are spread for shelter from the sun. The emperor is there with all his escort. And in the front row is a man wearing a toga with the purple stripe which marks him a senator sitting with another man in the simple brown habit of a desert monk. Two gladiators fight: one falls: the crowd gives the thumbs down sign: the emperor follows them, and a lifeless corpse is dragged away. Two more come out. It is too much for the monk. He vaults the barrier, pushes the fighters apart, pulls a crucifix from his rope belt and cries "Not in my name but in his I bid you stop!"

They cut him down amid the jeers of the crowd whose cruel sport he had dared to interrupt. But God moves in a mysterious way his wonders to perform. That was the last gladiatorial show ever held in Rome. One man, Telemachus, acted in love, suffered, and changed the world.

Source: Theodoret *Church History*

16 Francis of Assisi

Pietro Bernadone's son Giovanni was born at Assisi in the early 1180s while his father was on a business trip to France, as a result of which he gave his son the additional name of Francesco, by which posterity has known him. Francis grew up as a young-man-about-town, and something of a trial to his father. Life as a prisoner-of-war broke his idle ways. Released, he returned to them. Illness brought the first crisis of conversion. The second came from a pilgrimage to Rome. The religious life of the capital touched him not at all, except to realize that the pilgrims who claimed so much were giving so little. What moved him was the spectacle of hordes of beggars. He began to ask whether the call of God was not merely to succour suffering humanity but to take their burden upon himself and be identified with them.

From this point he turned from his earthly father to his heavenly Father. He stripped himself of all possessions, and went out to labour in his Father's vineyard. He sustained himself by manual labour or through alms; his real work was to preach the gospel of joy and love and peace in the midst of a world where lust for power reigned, and men were as wolves to one another. How could this be?

First because his life was God-centred, and he saw God in Jesus Christ sharing the sufferings of men. It is well known that Francis set up the first Christmas crib at Creccio. We tend to equate this with Albert bringing to Britain the first Christmas tree. The Christmas crib has become a sentimental prettiness for the children's corner of the church. It was not so to Francis. Here was a solemn and yet joyous message—to children, for he loved children, and to ordinary worshippers, but also to episcopal potentates and learned theologians: "Behold your God, a poor and helpless child, with ox and ass at his side."

This gave him his vision of perfect joy. Not holiness, not the gift of healing, not prophecy, not the understanding of God's world, not even the power to preach so as to change men's lives. This is perfect joy—to share the sufferings of the world, as Christ did: "When we arrive at Santa Maria degli Angeli, soaked with rain, frozen with cold, covered with mud, dying of hunger, and we knock and the porter comes in a rage, saying, 'Who are you?' and we answer, 'We are two of your brethren,' and he says, 'You lie, you are two lewd fellows who go up and down corrupting the world and stealing the alms of the poor. Go away from here!' and he does not open to us, but leaves us outside shivering in the snow and rain, frozen, starved, till night; then, if thus maltreated and turned away, we patiently endure all without murmuring against him, if we think with humility and charity that this porter really knows us truly and that God makes him speak thus to us, then, Brother Leo, write that in this is the perfect joy."

From this came Francis's deep sense of brotherhood which led him, in response to his Master's example, to identify himself with others. The rich merchant's son had wedded his Lady Poverty; and his proudest title was *poverello*, the little poor man. He identified himself with the leper by kissing his wounds. The wolf was his brother; death was his sister. *The Canticle of the Sun* is his hymn of praise in words, but first he lived it.

This was the age of the Crusaders, when European Christendom tried to avoid internecine strife by directing their armies against the Muslims. That was not the way of Francis. Three times he went out with the Crusaders—the only man among them fit to wear the Cross—not to kill the Saracens but to preach to them. Twice he was repulsed. The third time he deliberately got himself captured and went to the Sultan in fearless love to tell him of Christ. The Sultan listened with courtesy and sent him back unharmed.

But how to transform a world of war, and power, and cruelty, and hatred, and worldly wisdom, and "political realism"? There was the message—the message to those in power that the Son of Man came not to be ministered to, but to minister; the message to war-crazy petty principalities and embattled Christendom that the climactic title of the child in the manger was "Prince of Peace" and that this Prince of Peace blessed the peacemakers, condemned the works of the sword and entrusted to his followers the ministry of reconciliation; the message to those who hated their fellows that, in being born a man, Christ made all men his brothers, and brothers of one another; the message that God had created all creatures and all men to be brothers, and that if he could have a wolf for his friend, surely human beings could love one another. But the message alone was not enough. In Francis's renunciation of the world there was something of the old Cynic attitude. Possessions do disturb the peace of mind; Jesus said it, as well as Diogenes. When the Bishop of Assisi said that he thought that to lack possessions must be a harsh and difficult way of life, Francis rejoined, "My lord, if we possessed property we should have need of arms for its defence, for it is the source of quarrels and lawsuits, and the love of God and of one's neighbour usually finds many obstacles therein; this is why we do not desire temporal goods." The man who was unburdened by possessions was set free to love and to joy in the life of love. But the whole burden must go, and Francis would not claim for himself, did not allow the brethren to claim, and in his testament continued to forbid any protection of any kind from the Roman *curia*. In this way freedom from possessions was exposure to the worst the world could do. Francis knew this; in one sense he renounced the world, in another he embraced it. He laid no claims upon it, but he allowed it to claim him. He knew that to transform, to redeem the world required a heart ready to accept the world in its entirety, and to offer itself as an unsullied sacrifice. It was to take up the Cross.

The *stigmata* are in fact central to our understanding of Francis. We are learning more about the power of mind over matter, and there is nothing for the rationalist to doubt, while to the faithful they remain a miracle, because the gift of God. During the 1939-45 War, a man was brutally bound and maltreated by the Gestapo and left for dead. He was nursed back to some measure of physical health but remained a neurotic wreck. In seeking to help him, they hypnotized him and asked him to project himself back to the prison-camp. Immediately, the deep weals of the ropes appeared on his wrists and ankles. Francis spent a lifetime in contemplation of Christ crucified. His service of man was his Master's. His way of transforming the world by sacrificial love was his Master's. He was in Christ. He was making up that which was lacking to the sufferings of Christ. Towards the end of his life, marks corresponding to the five wounds of Christ appeared on his body. There was no exhibitionism in Francis. He kept the manifestation dark from even his most intimate disciples. But they meant much to him, and he died with his left hand upon the wound in his side, saying, "I have done what I had to do; may Christ teach you what is your part."

Source: J. Ferguson *The Place of Suffering*

17 George Fox (1624–91)

George Fox lived through a stormy period of political upheaval and religious questioning.

His parents were religious folk, but even they found him hard to understand. In his *Journal* he records that at eleven years "the Lord taught me to be faithful in all things and to act faithfully two ways, namely, inwardly to God and outwardly to man; and to keep to yea and nay in all things." The essence of the Society of Friends is there.

He received a call from God to forsake all. He found no help from the established church nor from the dissenters. God was not to be found in universities or churches, but in the hearts of people. So he set out on his travels to proclaim the call of Jesus. He was in and out of prison, though he was liable to convert those who arrested him. Soon Quakerism, as it came to be called, was a movement, with meetings up and down the country. There were partners in the work now, notably Margaret Fell, whom he married in 1669. He himself travelled further afield—to America and to Europe. To the last he was preaching and praying. A day or two before his death he said, "I am clear, I am fully clear."

He was a striking figure, with his long hair, penetrating eyes, leather breeches, and broad-brimmed hat and loud voice.

Part of his understanding of the gospel was that it was contrary to the teaching of Jesus to fight with "carnal weapons" or to strike one's enemies, as indeed it is. But Fox, unlike many Christians, practised what his Lord preached.

In a remarkable episode early in his life he was in prison in 1651 in Derby. The soldiers were recruiting for Cromwell's army. They haled him out of prison, asking if he would not take up arms for the commonwealth against Charles Stuart, and offering him a captaincy. "I told them I knew from whence all wars arose, even from the lusts, according to James's doctrine, and that I lived in the virtue of that life and power that took away the occasion of all wars" and that "I was come into the covenant of peace which was before wars and strifes were."

He did not prescribe other people's conscience. William Penn as a gentleman, after his conversion, continued to wear his sword. He asked Fox about this. The advice was, "Wear it as long as thou canst." The sword soon disappeared. On the other hand, he would not suffer violence to be used in his defence, and when a soldier came to his rescue in Ulverston market Fox caught his sword-hand and "bid him put up his sword again if he would go along with me."

Fox constantly demonstrated the power of suffering love. A drunken prisoner in Scarborough challenged him to a fight. Fox waited until he was sober; then "seeing he had challenged me, I was now come to answer him, with my hands in my pockets, and (reaching my head towards him)'Here, ' said I 'is my hair, here are my cheeks, here is my back.' " The other slunk away, conquered without a blow.

Nor was he slow to intervene when others were at blows. In Hertfordshire he intervened in a desperate fight, held the two combatants apart one in each hand, "showed them the evil of their doing and reconciled them one to the other; and they were so loving and thankful to me that people wondered at it."

Fox showed the power of passive resistance—not in the sense of doing nothing—he was active in intervention—but in the constant readiness to suffer rather than to inflict suffering. Some early Friends had been in the army (and this has led some historians who ought to know better to play down the nonviolence of the early movement). Fox's own witness was strong; others had to be convicted by their own Inward Light, and sometimes it came hard. But there are many accounts of the steadfast refusal of the Quakers to meet with violence the violence to which they were constantly exposed.

The soldiers at Scarborough who were his jailers paid George Fox a rare tribute when they said "He is as stiff as a tree and as pure as a bell."

Sources: George Fox, *Journal*; Thomas Hodgkin, *George Fox*; Vernon Noble, *George Fox*; Geoffrey Nuttall, *Christian Pacifism in History*; *Reconciliation Quarterly*, Dec. 1980

18 Leonard Fell

Leonard Fell, one of the early Quakers, was victim of a hold-up. The highwayman demanded his money, which he handed over. The highwayman then required his horse. Leonard Fell dismounted, and let him take it. Then, feeling the power of truth rise in his mind, he solemnly warned the robber of the evil of his ways. The other flew into a passion, asked the Friend why he preached to him, and threatened to blow out his brains. Leonard Fell replied, "Though I would not give my life for my money or my horse, I would give it to save thy soul." The highwayman was taken quite aback, and said that if he was such a man as that he would take neither his money nor his horse from him, and returned both.

Source: George Fox, *Journal*

19 John Sharpe (1645 – 1714)

John Sharpe, a friend of Queen Anne, was Archbishop of York for nearly a quarter of a century. After he became Archbishop he was victim of a hold-up on the road by a bandit armed with a pistol. The Archbishop spoke gently to him and in a Christian Spirit, and asked about his need. He explained that he was in desperate need of fifty pounds. The Archbishop gave him what he had about him and promised to make up the rest of the sum if the bandit would come to the palace next day. The man came and the Archbishop welcomed him and gave him the rest of the promised money. Eighteen months later the man returned to repay the money. His fortunes had taken a turn for the better, and through the "astonishing goodness" of the Archbishop he had become "the most penitent, the most grateful, and happiest of his species".

Jonathan Dymond (1796 – 1828), who tells the story in his *Principles of Morality*, comments, "Let the reader consider how different the Archbishop's feelings were, from what they would have been if by his hand, this man had been cut off."

Source: Jonathan Dymond, *Principles of Morality*

20 John Wesley at Falmouth

At Falmouth on 4 July 1745, Wesley faced a mob crying for his blood. He was visiting a sick woman. The mob cried, "Bring out the Canorum! Where is the Canorum?" Canorum was a Cornish word for canter. The mob, reinforced by a gang of sailors, broke in the outer door. "O sir, what must we do?" said one of the women. "We must pray," said Wesley, and added in his diary, "Indeed, at that time, to all appearance, our lives were not worth an hour's purchase." She suggested that he should hide. He replied, "No. It is best for me to stand just where I am."

The mob smashed in the inner door, and fell back in astonishment as Wesley, unarmed, bareheaded to be sure of being recognized, stepped out calmly with the words "Here I am. Which of you has anything to say to me? To which of you have I done any wrong? To you? Or you?" As he spoke, without their realizing what was happening, he led them back out from the house into the street. Once outside he raised his voice: "Neighbours, countrymen! Do you desire to hear me speak?" Mobs can be fickle. "Yes, yes," they cried vehemently. "He shall speak. He shall. Nobody shall hinder him." The crowd fell silent, and though he had no platform to speak from, so that his voice did not carry to the back, they heard him out, and some of the leaders of the mob turned to their followers and swore that no-one should touch him.

Source: John Wesley, *Journal*

21 William Rotch (18th century)

William Rotch was a member of the Society of Friends, living on the island of Nantucket during the War of American Independence. The war hit the islanders hard. Because of the British Navy they were no longer able to pursue their avocation of whaling. Further, the island was open to plunder and privateering.

One day a British warship sailed into the harbour, heavy with guns. A boat put out to shore with an officer on board. William Rotch met him on the quayside, shook hands and said "I would like thee to come to my house." The officer was surprised at this welcome, but, supposing the man to be a British loyalist, accepted. It was about mid-day. William said "I would like thee to take dinner with me." They enjoyed a pleasant meal, and eventually the officer thought he should get down to business, and said to the presumed loyalist, "I came here for plunder and I would like you to tell me, as a friend, how and where I had better begin." The answer was even more unexpected. "I don't know any better place for thee to begin than here at my house, for I am better able to bear the loss than anyone else." The officer stared at him. "Are there any more men like you on this island?" he asked. "Yes, there are many better men than I am here." "I should like to see some of them." "Well, I will introduce thee to some of our leading citizens." He took the officer into a store and said "This man distributed four hundred barrels of flour among the poor of the island last winter." They went out in silence. In each store he was able to tell some similar act of well doing. At the end the officer shook hands with William, and said, meaning the word literally, "Farewell." He took to the boat, and the ship sailed away.

Source: A Ruth Fry, *Victories without Violence*

33

22 Abby Greene
(18th century)

During the American War of Independence, a Quaker woman named Abby Greene had a husband of somewhat violent inclinations, who sided with the fight for independence. Advised that the British were going to burn down her house, Abby persuaded her husband to keep out of the way, and as the officer advanced with a lighted torch greeted him with the words, "I hope you have not come to do us any harm? Come in, I will get you something to eat." The officer stared at her for a moment, then extinguished his torch with the words "Dear old mother, we won't hurt a hair of your head," and, with his men, came in to share the meal.

Source: Amelia Gummere, *Quakers in the Forum*

23 Jacob, Elizabeth and Dinah Goff (1798)

Jacob and Elizabeth Goff were Irish members of the Society of Friends. Dinah was one of their twenty-two children. In 1857, she wrote *Divine Protection through Extraordinary Dangers* in which she told the story of their experiences in the so-called Irish Rebellion fifty-nine years before, when she was fourteen.

The Goffs lived in County Wexford, where the violence was at its height. Their house was situated between two of the insurgent camps, whose soldiers would descend upon them and "liberate" their food-stocks and horses. Battles were fought around them. On one occasion the artillery was directed so as to blow up their house, but the military were told that they were not rebels but Quakers and never fired. The grounds were a refugee camp. Each day they fed hundreds of people, and Dinah and her sisters were responsible for their welfare, hearing all the time horrific stories of violence and torture.

One day a squad of soldiers appeared with a black flag. It was the signal of death. Jacob and Elizabeth walked, unarmed and unprotected, towards the soldiers as they prepared their muskets. They reached the soldiers, faced them and said, "Why do you not begin?" "We cannot," was the shamefaced reply.

Later the house was raided by an armed mob looting for money. Twice Jacob's life was at stake. The first time he was saved by his eldest daughter, the second by Dinah herself. It was the girls' willingness to die with their father which saved him from the mob.

Source: Dinah Goff, *Divine Protection through Extraordinary Dangers*

24 John Nelson (c. 1800)

John Nelson was a Methodist. The rules of the Methodists required them to be "in every kind merciful after their power" and to do "good of every possible sort, and as far as possible, to all men".

England was at war with France. Nelson was press-ganged. True to his understanding of the way of Christ, he refused to become a soldier. They castigated and chastised him, flung him into prisons, forced him to march from place to place. Still he proclaimed the way of Christ.

"A court-martial was held, and I was guarded to it by a file of musketeers, with their bayonets fixed. When I came before the court, they asked, 'What is this man's crime?' The answer was, 'This is the Methodist preacher, and he refuses to take money.' Then they turned to me, and said, 'Sir, you need not find fault with us, for we must obey orders, which are to make you act as a soldier; for you are delivered to us; and if you have not justice done you, we cannot help it.' My answer was 'I shall not fight; for I cannot bow the knee before the Lord to pray for a man, and get up and kill him when I have done.' Next morning I was ordered to parade. The officers ordered Captain W. to fetch me a gun and other war-like instruments. I asked, 'Why do you gird me with these war-like habiliments? for I am a man averse to war, and shall not fight, but under the Prince of Peace, the Captain of my salvation; and the weapons He gives me are not carnal like these.' "

At Sunderland the officers said they would make him wear clothing belonging to a soldier. Nelson answered, "You may array me as a man of war, but I shall never fight." "They asked me, 'What is your reason?' My answer was, 'I cannot see anything in this world worth fighting for. I want neither its riches nor honours, but the honour that cometh from God only.' "

Friends procured his release. As he departed he repeated his understanding of the gospel to the officer in charge. "Well," said the officer, "if you be so scrupulous about fighting, what must *we* do?" Nelson answered, "It is your trade; and if you had a better, it might be better for you." "But somebody must fight." "If all men lived by faith in the Son of God, wars would be at an end." "That is true, if it were so, we should learn war no more."

Source: Henry Carter, *A Study in Discipleship*

25 Elizabeth Fry

Elizabeth Gurney was born in Norfolk of a well-known Quaker family, and married Joseph Fry in 1800. By 1809 she knew that she was called to public ministry. Four years later her interest in prison reform began.

It was in January 1817 that Elizabeth first made her way to Newgate. The turnkeys would not let her in. They themselves never went in alone. While they were arguing, one of the women inside made for the others, snatched their caps, was ready enough to claw and scratch. But Elizabeth had her pass and her determination. Their intentions were good, but she was going in alone. She was wearing a watch as the only ornament on her plain Quaker dress. They pleaded with her to leave it behind. "Oh no, I thank you. My watch goes with me everywhere. I am not afraid. Open the gate for me, please!"

They pushed the gate open and it clanged behind her. Inside there was a moment's shocked astonishment before the crowd surged forward. But there was something about her which prevented them from molesting her. More, her habit marked her as religious, and the prisoners, whatever they might have done, had a sense of religion.

Elizabeth had not planned what to do; she relied on the Inward Light, on the guidance of the Spirit, on the presence of Jesus. She picked up a grubby child, and said "Friends, many of you are mothers. I too am a mother. I am distressed for your children. Is there not something we can do for these little innocent ones? Do you want them to grow up to become real prisoners themselves? Are they to learn to become thieves and worse?"

They listened. They brought her a chair. They brought their children to her, as eighteen centuries before people had brought children to Jesus. For hours they poured out their stories to her. When eventually she departed, she left behind a new spirit — Hope.

On one occasion Elizabeth was staying in a hotel in Bristol in the course of her prison work, when she noticed a man's boot sticking out from under the bed. Totally unafraid, she knelt by the bed and began to pray for the intruder. He crept out and knelt beside her. When she had done she turned to him and said "And now, friend, tell me what brought thee hither?" He told her how starvation had tempted him to steal. She talked with him, found him to be genuine, escorted him to the door of the hotel so that he could leave unchallenged, and helped him in practical ways.

Source: Janet Whitney, *Elizabeth Fry*

26 The Martyrs of Madagascar

Christian missionaries reached Madagascar in 1818. By 1831 it was estimated that there were some two thousand converts, and that perhaps 30,000 of the islanders had come within range of Christian influence. But in 1835 there came to the throne Queen Ranavalone I, and there followed more than a quarter of a century of bitter and largely unremitting persecution. In 1839 the order was given that all Christians should be seized, bound, thrown in a pit, should have boiling water poured over them and should be buried on the spot. Again in 1849 there were eighteen death sentences, and over 2,000 Christians were sentenced to other penalties such as flogging and enslavement. Yet the Christians stood firm. The cruel queen herself was moved to astonished and reluctant admiration. "I have killed some, " she said, "I have made some slaves till death, I have put some in long and heavy fetters, and still you continue praying. How is it that you cannot give that up?" Her very officers used to say to one another, "Let us go and see how these Christians behave; they are not afraid to die." A spectator who watched some Christians at the stake in 1849 left his record: "They prayed as long as they had life. Then they died, but softly, gently. Indeed, gentle was the going forth of their life, and astonished were all the people around that beheld the burning of them."

In 1861 the queen died, and her successor Radama II proclaimed religious liberty. From bush and forest and wilderness and cave and mountain the Christians reappeared as if risen from the dead, and as they came back they sang the old pilgrim-song, "When the Lord turned again the captivity of Zion we were like them that dream." Then the incredible truth emerged. The Christians were many times more in number than they had been before the persecution started. The witness of the martyrs had borne fruit; their blood had proved to be seed.

Radama's successor Radavalona II was baptized in 1868, and in the following year destroyed the palace-idols, and commended Christianity to her people. There were already 50,000 members, and three times that number of adherents. Now there were 1,500,000 more hungry for the Word of Life.

Source: J. Ferguson, *The Place of Suffering*

27 William Hockett
(19th century)

William Hockett may be taken as representative of numerous conscientious objectors during the American Civil War. Col. Kirkland gave orders that he was to be shot. The commands were given "Load... Present arms... Aim..." Hockett raised his arms with the audible prayer "Father forgive them, for they know not what they do." The command was given "Fire," but not a finger was pressed on a trigger. Then came perhaps the most astonishing demonstration of the spirit of peace. One of the officers swore he would ride him down, but his horse refused. The man's heart was hardened, but something in that unfearing, unhating, ungrudging calmness reached through to the animal.

Source: A. Ruth Fry, *Victories without Violence*

28 Mosheu

Mosheu was an African chief converted to the Christian faith. The Christians were at prayer one Sunday morning, when a raiding-party from a neighbouring tribe appeared intent on plunder. Mosheu saw them approaching and rose with dignity telling his people to sit quietly and trust in God. He then went to meet the intruders and asked them what they wanted: "Your cattle, and if you raise a weapon to resist it is at your peril." "These are my cattle," said Mosheu tranquilly, and went to rejoin the worshippers. They sang a hymn, read a passage of scripture, then knelt in prayer. The raiding-party, who had come for rapine and plunder, were overawed by this spectacle of calm faith, and withdrew, their violent purposes unfulfilled.

Source: Robert Moffat *Missionary Labours and Scenes in Southern Africa*

29 Joshua Hart

In the mangrove swamps near the coast of Nigeria, there is a town called Bonny. A hundred and twenty years ago it was a sinister place, rich, but cruel and superstitious; it was still a centre of slavery; not long before, it had been a centre of the slave-trade. There came Christian preachers with the message of God's love in Jesus. One convert, a boy, was given the name Joshua as his Christian name. He was a slave to a cruel owner, a chief known as Captain Hart. Captain Hart tried to make him eat meat which had been offered to idols; Joshua refused. He was punished for disobeying. Still he refused. The threw him high in the air, and let him fall on the hard ground. His body was bruised and broken; his spirit was strong. He said "If my master requires me to work for him, however hard, I will try my best to do it. But if he requires me to partake of things sacrificed to the gods, I will never do it."

Now Joshua was condemned to death. Tied hand and foot he was taken out in a canoe to be drowned. As he went he prayed Jesus's own prayer: "Forgive them for they know not what they do." "You be praying again?" cried Captain Hart and flung him, helpless as he was, into the water. They fished him out with a boathook, and gave him a last chance. He was still firm. They threw him in again to die.

Centuries before an African named Tertullian had watched the courage of Christians in facing death. They died, but their courage persuaded others of their faith. "The blood of Christians is seed," said Tertullian. In Bonny, persecution went on for three years. The Christians fled to the "bush", the thick, wild forest. But something was happening to Captain Hart, just as it had happened to the persecutor Saul of Tarsus, the apostle Paul, in the early days of the Church. It was he who pleaded for freedom of worship. When the Christians came out from hiding, they were more in number than they had been. And one of the first people to ask for baptism was Captain Hart.

Source: J. Ferguson, *Nigerian Church Founders*

30 Lucretia Mott

The Annual Meeting of the Anti-Slavery Society was being held in New York. Among those present were such notable figures as William Lloyd Garrison and John Greenleaf Whittier. The meeting was broken up by a hostile gang of toughs. Some of the speakers, who included a number of women, were being roughly handled. Lucretia Mott asked the man escorting her to go to the help of some of the other women. "But who will take care of you?" he asked. She turned to one of the roughnecks, put her hand on his arm, and said, "This man; he will see me safe through." The man looked astonished, opened his mouth, closed it again, and escorted her to safety. Next day at a restaurant nearby she recognized the leader of the gang and went straight over to him and talked to him. After she had gone he asked what was the lady's name. "Lucretia Mott." "Well," he said, "She's a good sensible woman."

Source: James and Lucretia Mott, *Life and Letters*

31 Mary Slessor

Mary Slessor grew up in a rough part of Glasgow, the child of a shoe-maker who was also a drunkard. She had a harsh childhood and began factory work at the age of eleven. But she had a Christian upbringing and she was still quite young when she began herself to bring her faith to others. She would speak in the open air, the true witness, *kerygma* or proclamation. One day a gang of young toughs came at her. One had a lead weight on a string which he whirled closer and ever closer to her head. She never flinched. ''She's game, boys,'' he said, and they listened to what she had to say. She won them for Christ by her courage.

She was twenty-eight when she went as a missionary to Calabar in West Africa where she settled among fierce tribes. The peoples of the Cross River regarded twins as accursed and left them to die. Mary rescued, and brought them up. She had no children of her own but was a mother to many.

Her unarmed courage saved the people time and again from violence. On one occasion a chief's son had been killed by accident. She knew there would be reprisals. Witchcraft pointed to the guilt of one village, and some twelve people including three women with babies were brought for execution. Their armed captors, dancing with spears and guns, intoxicated with rum, went wild. Mary watched by the prisoners and would not let them be taken to death. One woman she released herself. Others the chiefs released for her sake. In the end she saved them all.

One of the practices of the Calabar area was the poison ordeal, by which a man ate poison beans to show his guilt or innocence. The chief's brother was charged with his nephew's death. He was resolved on the ordeal. Mary went to stop him and confiscate the beans. He said that he had none, but she found them and took them. A little later, hearing a noise, she went out and found the chief, mad drunk, with a bag. She demanded it with quiet authority. He flung it at her. She found forty beans at the bottom. ''I'll take the liberty of keeping these,'' she said. He protested. She held on to the bag and walked away between two lines of armed men, daring them to take the bag from her.

On another occasion the drums were beating for war. As the two tribal armies advanced, she stood between them. She would not move until the soldiers laid down their arms on either side of her in piles which reached to a height of five feet.

There was a similar occasion when, although due for leave, she heard of the danger of a war and went straight to the place. The chief said "I know of no war but if there were a war, a woman would be no use." Mary replied, "In measuring the woman's power, you have evidently forgotten to take into account the woman's God." She eventually found where the trouble was, and in good round Scots bluntness told them not to be fools. A wall of armed men confronted her. They made no response. She gave no way. Then an old chief whom she had helped suddenly flung himself at her feet and admitted that he had wounded the chief on the other side, and asked her to use her good offices for peace. She called together leaders on both sides, and she herself knelt before them and pleaded for a peaceable outcome. The tribes felt this to be cowardice; war was the only manly way of settling things. She persisted. The dispute was resolved by a fine, and her authority was such that she could go on leave knowing that the agreement would be honoured.

On one occasion she was accidentally struck in a brawl. Both sides would have killed the offender, had she not intervened on his behalf. This was the only occasion on which violence was ever offered against her person.

Source: W. P. Livingstone, *Mary Slessor of Calabar*

32 Theodore Pennell

Theodore Pennell came to the north-west frontier of India in 1892 as a Christian medical missionary. It was an area of violence, warfare and banditry. Dr. Pennell was a man of peace. He travelled unarmed. He was there to save life, not to take it. He lived among the people as one of them, wearing their dress, speaking their tongue. They met him with suspicion; he healed their illnesses, asked for no payment, and was never too weary to help those in need.

Some of the Mullahs declared that his death was a religious duty for a follower of the Prophet. One of them sent out a company of young fanatics to kill him. Pennell rode unarmed into the Mullah's village at the end of his day's work in the hospital, to ask why he had issued such an order. The Mullah could not understand his fearlessness, but with the characteristic hospitality of a Muslim and a Pathan, offered him a meal. By tradition, once Pennell had broken bread with him, he was under his host's protection. But in conversation Pennell won over the Mullah to see the service he could give to the Mullah's people. Presently Pennel said that he was tired, and asked to sleep. He lay down and went straight to sleep. The Mullah's assassins said "Now is our chance to kill him." "He is my guest."'"But not ours." "Well, look at him, he is alone and unarmed among declared enemies, and yet he sleeps with absolute calm. Could we kill a man of such courage?" So Pennell's courage and trustfulness won his enemies.

On another occasion he was invited to give medical help to an army of two thousand outlaws under a bandit named Chikki, whose own men came to escort him. He refused a British escort, and travelled alone and unarmed. Chikki actually organized and 'chaired' a discussion between Pennell and the local Mullah. Chikki became Pennell's personal friend and, when war broke out, refused to allow his troops, and others over which he had influence, to join in. The result was that peace was speedily restored.

Pennell was a man of peace, who spread peace. A famous Commander-in-Chief is reported to have said that Pennell was worth two regiments on the Frontier.

Source: Mrs. Pennell in A. Ruth Fry, *Victories without Violence*

33 Roland Hayes

In the early years of this century, Roland Hayes, the Negro singer, was brutally set upon late one night by four white policemen. He was in the obvious sense defenceless; there was no help near.

"I was no match physically for even one of them. But I *was* a match for them in another way, and so was able to overcome them. I brought to bear a power that no evil can stand against. I retired into God-consciousness. I just prayed for the spirit of Christ to flow through me into the hearts of those misguided men. As I thus exercised spiritual thought-power, suddenly I had a feeling of being lifted high above this hatred, and I looked down upon them in compassion and pity. One policeman raised his pistol with the intent of hitting me with its butt. While his arm was raised a curious and bewildered expression came over his face. Slowly his poised arm dropped. He had been stopped by the tremendous power of the spirit, by God-consciousness."

Source: Roland Hayes reported in, *A Guide to Confident Living*

34 The Russian Mennonite

I cannot give the name of the family concerned in this episode.
The story was told privately by the son in 1938. The episode took
place in Southern Russia during the 1905 revolution. Insurgent
groups were sweeping the country, killing and destroying. The
Mennonite family were approached by their neighbours. "Tell
me, friend, what will you do when they come? Are you suffi-
ciently armed? My six sons and I have guns, so we will be able
to defend ourselves. We'll shoot them." "We have no arms in
the house. I do not believe in this kind of defence; there is no
certainty in it." "Well, don't blame me for what will happen to
you when they come!"

The next day the news came that, for all their guns, the
neighbours had been massacred, and their home looted and
burned. The Mennonites knew it would be their turn next.

The father showed no fear. He told his wife to prepare a
good supper for their guests and beds for about ten people. He
then disappeared. The children eventually found him by peering
through the keyhole of a locked room. He was kneeling in prayer.

He waited until they heard heavy steps and a voice calling
"Hands up and surrender." The father went out and took the
leader—there were twelve in the gang—by the hand saying
"Come in. Everything that is ours is yours, but first come in and
refresh yourselves. The supper is ready."

The men muttered. "Don't let's let him cheat us. We came
to kill him, not to eat with him."

"I know," came the reply. "Come and eat first, then you
can do whatever you think is right to do."

They came in suspiciously, and sat in silence. They were
hungry and exhausted. The food was enticing. The man sat with
them. "Eat, eat, everything is yours. Your beds are prepared in
the next room. You certainly need a good rest."

They did, and they took it. When he woke up, the leader, a
man of wild, fierce appearance, said with a smile: "We have to
go. We came to kill you, but we can't."

Source: Enrico Molnar in A.A. Hunter, *Courage in Both Hands*

51

35 Patrick Lloyd

The story of Pat Lloyd, a man of more than usual Irish pugnacity, is one of the more remarkable stories of the First World War. Pugnacious, patriotic and popular, he lied about his age in order to join the Canadian army at the age of seventeen. The experience of the carnage in France overwhelmed him. It was not that he was afraid, but that the waste of human lives in the churned-up mud was so appalling. He was in the front line carrying on his head some sheets of corrugated iron. Shells were bursting around. He rested for a moment. It all seemed meaningless. Suddenly he became aware of a brilliant figure approaching. The figure paused for a moment, gently shook his head, smiled and passed on. Pat was certain he had been in the presence of Jesus Christ. He was equally certain that that shaking of the head meant that he could never in the future kill.

He went and told his colonel, who said "What the hell do you think we're here for?" He was court-martialed, tried, and condemned to death. But Pat was respected and the colonel was reluctant to carry out the sentence.

Pat sat very still in prayer. Then he went to the colonel, and said that he was prepared to obey Army Regulations in every way except killing. The colonel checked Army Regulations and observed that capital offences were cowardice in the face of the enemy and throwing away arms in face of the enemy. So Pat went "over the top" in the forefront of his company, but refused to use his arms. When an unpopular sergeant-major ordered him to shoot, he tried to avoid a confrontation in which the others would have been on his side; he simply shot harmlessly high and wide. On one occasion he came back with sixteen bullet-holes in his uniform. Apart from a graze he was himself untouched. His courage was such that the colonel, who had a sense of humour, promoted him from corporal to sergeant.

On one occasion Pat had gone into the German trenches with his rifle slung over his shoulder, when a German came round the corner of the trench with rifle and bayonet at the ready. Pat extended his hands in a gesture of friendship, and walked towards the German saying *"Kamerad!"* which of course does not mean "I surrender" but "Friend!" The German kept his bayonet to the fore. Pat went on: *"Sprechen sie deutsch?* You *sprechen* English?" The German was patently puzzled and replied *"Nein* English."

Pat's German was limited but he managed *"Liebe mannen, alles mannen."* *"Alles mannen? Deutsch?"* asked the German incredulously. *"Ja, alles mannen"* said Pat, and balanced his rifle harmlessly flat on his hands.

The German realized that there was nothing to fear. They sat down side by side on a step. Pat did not know the German for war. He tried *"Nicht* war." The German looked puzzled. Pat tried *"Nicht la guerre."* At the sound of the French language the German spat. So Pat repeated in an impeccable Irish-Canadian-German accent that he loved all men.

This was too much for the German who burst into a great roar of laughter, waved his rifle in the air, and cried *"Ach! Freund! Freund!"*

So they sat talking, each in his own language, not understanding the words, but communicating friendship, until the time came for them to part.

Pat Lloyd carried the same spirit into peace. After the war he was working among the needy in the slums of London. One unemployed drunkard was bitter with him. Pat thought it better to be silent. The man burst out "Bugger you, stop loving me!" But Pat did not. A few days later he pressed into the man's hand an address where he might find work. There was an amusing and ironical repercussion. The man, drinking in a bar, heard someone criticizing Pat and promptly knocked him down.

On another occasion, Pat was awakened by an armed burglar demanding his money. Pat said he had not much, and he needed it, but would share it. He gave the man food, and persuaded him to leave his gun behind because of the trouble if he were caught, though he failed to persuade him to come to him for honest work.

On yet another occasion he was a student counsellor, helping students to react constructively to situations of tension. Someone spat in his face. All Pat's Irish paddy was aroused, and his fists began to clench, but he kept himself under control and simply said in quiet tones "Would you lend me your handkerchief?" The man was dumbfounded, and did so, and as Pat mopped his face he began to blush so red that Pat himself was embarrassed.

Such was Pat Lloyd, the soldier who refused to kill.

Source: Allan Hunter, *Courage in Both Hands*

36 Edward Richards

Ned Richards was an American and a conscientious objector in the First World War. He stated that "absolute power and absolute love as combined in the character of Jesus Christ are a fundamental fact, in which the man who is trying to follow Christ can trust. In other words, the man following Christ can rely upon a Divine Power which has power over all things. This Divine Power is fundamentally the power of utter love." The person who commits himself to Christ must be ready to be killed, as soldiers were, without killing, as they did. The force of love is the only power strong enough to overcome evil.

Ned Richards felt that he had been sheltered from the dangers of the war and he should test his faith by serving in a situation of violence. He went to Western Iran, an area of disease, warfare, violence, racial and national hatreds, religious fanaticism, banditry, massacres, deprivation. He was in charge of industrial relief. He depicted the situation: "The ill-will stirred up by the war, the persecutions, the massacres, the assaulting of women, and the carrying off of girls, had intensified to a terrible degree the age-long hatred between the Syrians and the Armenians on the one hand, and the Kurds, Turks, and Moslems on the other. There were thousands of people who had been driven from their homes, and were refugees."

Ned Richards was in a room of the mission compound with the women and children and one invalid man. A group of armed Kurds arrived and crashed on the door with their rifle-butts. Ned Richards loosened the bolt and welcomed them, saying, "Come in." They had their rifles at the ready, but were taken aback at being admitted. They demanded money. He took them past the women and children to the study and Dr. Dodd, the invalid, handed over the small change. But the safe was locked.

"While the Kurds were rummaging about the room, I walked over to the safe that had the money in it and tried to open it. Like all Russian safes, it was an iron box with a lid like a trunk, the keyhole being in the top of the lid.

Finding the safe was locked, I stood there for a moment, and a horrible sinking feeling began to creep over me as the realisation of the situation came to me. There was nothing to do, however, but play the game, and so I turned back to the Kurds who were on the other side of the little room... as I turned, one of them suddenly threw up his rifle, covering me, and speaking in Turkish, demanded the key of the safe. Now I honestly did not have the key, and I looked him in the eye over the sights of the rifle, and told him so. Recognising that I was speaking the truth, he put his gun down and began to rummage round again.'' Richards felt he should go the second mile and suggested in sign-language that they might try to shoot out the lock. As the gun fired, they said to themselves in the next room, "There goes Richards. So much for Christian pacifism!'' But Richards had not gone. The lock did not budge. One of the Kurds hit him on the shoulder with his rifle butt. Richards looked at him in silence with an expression which said "What are you hitting me for? I am doing everything I can to help you.'' In the end the Kurds gave up, and left, harming no-one, and taking only a few clothes. One of the women said that if her husband had been there he would have tried to resist and they would all have been massacred. It was Ned Richards' fearless demonstration of nonviolent love in action which saved them.

On another occasion a young Armenian, drunk and armed, came into the yard to murder one of his enemies. Ned Richards thought that he should approach the man with friendliness and without fear. He managed to approach him before the man turned. The Armenian had his gun ready. "I smiled and held out my hand, offering to shake hands with him. Here was the test. I strove to appear to this poor drunken mind a friend who was not afraid. He swung round again and caught sight of me, hesitated a moment, and then, drawing himself up to attention, he grounded his rifle, and saluted me in unsteady drunken seriousness. As I came up close to him, I continued to hold out my hand, and much to my surprise, he handed me his gun, saying, as he did so, 'A present'. Taking the rifle in one hand and his arm in the other, I quietly walked with him to the gate.''

These are two stock situations in which many people suppose that active nonviolent love is impractical, protecting women and children against armed looters and confrontation with a crazy drunkard running amok with a lethal weapon. Ned Richards demonstrated the force of love.

Source: *Atlantic Monthly*, May 1923.

37 Miss Miller and the Bandits

Dr. Agnes Edmonds and Miss Miller were travelling by riverboat in China towards Chengtu, when they became aware that the boatmen were unnaturally silent as they rowed, and the captain was looking desperately anxious. They asked him the trouble, and he finally admitted: "Bandits have been killing and robbing in this district. They know you are on board and have been following for hours along the shore. And we must tie up at the next pier."

They tied up in silence. The captain produced a gun, the boatmen drew knives. Suddenly three armed bandits appeared.

"Captain! Put the gangplank down—I'm going ashore!" Miss Miller suddenly called. He protested, but she jumped ashore, and approached the bandits with a bow. Taken aback, they bowed in return. She smiled at them and said "Thank you, gentlemen." They looked puzzled. "We heard there were bandits in this country," said Miss Miller, "and we have been very frightened. Now we know we are safe, and we thank you for coming to protect us."

The leader, a giant of a man, turned to his companions with a broad grin. They grinned back and nodded. Then he said "We are gentlemen, as you say. There is nothing to fear. We will stand guard and you will be safe."

All night the company of eight or nine armed bandits guarded the boat they had come to raid, and waved it goodbye in the morning with bows and smiles.

Source: Dr. Agnes Edmonds, former head of
the Gamble Memorial Hospital, Chungking
in A. Ruth Fry, *Victories without Violence*

38 Toyohiko Kagawa

Kagawa was a Japanese Christian. At the age of twenty-one he went to live in the Shinkava slums of Tokyo, one of the most desperate and dangerous areas in the world. His room cost him about threepence (prewar) a day, cheap because a man had recently been murdered there, bug-ridden, tiny. All around were murderers, gangsters, madmen, drunkards, prostitutes. He loved them all and came to serve them.

Many times he faced death or injury. He met the threats with courage, love and humour. Once he was awakened by a drunken criminal standing over him with uplifted sword. Kagawa bowed in prayer and waited for the blow. Presently the man said "Kagawa, do you love me?" "Yes." There was silence for a moment. Then, "Here's a present," as the man handed over his sword.

A dangerous alcoholic had a love-hate relationship with him. On one occasion he came into Kagawa's room and began shaking the table. "Give me two yen or I'll shake it all day." "No," said Kagawa, "one's enough." On another occasion he demanded money for drink. Kagawa refused, and the man hit him, breaking four teeth. Even that Kagawa turned to a joke. To an English-speaking audience he would say "That's why I don't speak good English. The false teeth were put in by a Japanese dentist." He continued to share his food with the man. On another occasion the man, crazed with drink, went at Kagawa with a sword. Kagawa told bystanders not to intervene, and stood unarmed in a swordsman's pose, looking into the other's eyes, unwavering. So they stood for several minutes, till the other dropped his sword and went away.

On one occasion at a church service he was beaten up by a gang of toughs. He showed no fear or anger as he received the blows. When they had finished he led the congregation in prayer, and then invited the toughs to his study. As they talked together he won them over.

One of his greatest tests was when he heard that ten thousand angry strikers were marching towards a confrontation in the Kawasaki dockyards where armed soldiers were waiting for them. He dashed to intercept them, stood in their path, praying "Let there be peace," as he stared them straight in the face. They swerved off in another direction. Not a shot was fired. Kagawa was imprisoned for his pains.

Kagawa stood firmly against Japanese militarism, and wrote a poem asking the forgiveness of the Chinese for Japanese aggression. He suffered imprisonment and was nearly executed for his opposition to war.

He was a great believer in the Co-operative movement. After the war he gave his life to building up social service programmes, and to proclaiming his faith: "Love is power. Try it! Try it!"

Source: A. A. Hunter, *Three Trumpets Sound*

39 The Church of Jesus Christ on Earth through the Prophet Simon Kimbangu

Simon Kimbangu was born in the then Belgian Congo (later Zaire) in 1889. His parents died soon after; he was brought up by an aunt. In 1915, he was baptized into the Christian church. Three years later he heard a voice calling him to bear witness to Christ. In Christ's name he found he had the gift of healing, and it was certainly the view of his followers that the Holy Spirit had descended on him in a new Pentecost. He preached redemption by Christ for Whites and Blacks alike. Many flocked to his home in N'Kamba. Some false prophets exploited the situation.

By 1921, the Belgian administration were scared. They tried to arrest him. The soldiers behaved brutally to peaceful villagers and killed a child. Simon and his close associates escaped. No-one betrayed them. Then he heard God's voice "Return to N'Kamba to be arrested." He did so, told his followers to face suffering courageously, not to use violence and not to repay evil for evil; he then gave himself freely to the soldiers. He was put in chains, and three weeks later was sentenced by a court-martial to one hundred and twenty lashes and then to be put to death. The charges were rebellion, endangering the security of the state, and outrageous action towards an officer in pursuance of his duty. The charges were trumped up, and no witnesses or counsel for the defence were allowed. Kimbangu bore himself with great dignity. As a result of representations from the missionary societies the sentence was commuted to life imprisonment. His behaviour in prison was so exemplary that, in 1935, the governor recommended his release. This was not granted. Simon Kimbangu died in prison on 12 October 1951.

Meantime his followers suffered persecution and deportation. This had an effect contrary to that intended. The new movement spread far beyond its original home. In the intense persecution of 1925, they continued to gather in secret, sing hymns of hope, believing that they were suffering with Jesus, pray for forgiveness, and show no hatred to their persecutors.

The Church continued to spread. Marie-Louise Martin estimated three million members in 1970. During a time of increased violence in 1964, the Kimbanguists neither fled nor retaliated. They were ready to die but not to kill. They prayed. Soldiers burst in on them. "What are you doing?" "Praying." "Yes, praying for the rebels." "We're praying for all God's children and for peace." They were left unharmed.

In 1960, the Church introduced new statutes declaring that they teach: (a) love, worship, mercy and imitation of Christ; (b) abhorrence of evil and love of all that is good; (c) justice and moral purity; (d) every religious practice which serves the cultivation of mutual respect and unity between people and nations, which comprise the essential basis for harmony and peace in the world. In 1969 the Church was admitted to the World Council for Churches.

The story of Simon Kimbangu and his followers is a wonderful story of commitment to nonviolent love in the Spirit of Christ, faithfulness in suffering, and growth through faithfulness in despite of persecution.

Sources: Marie-Louise Martin, *Kimbangu* (1975); Jean Lasserre, *Cahiers de la Réconciliation*, May-June 1946; Lanza del Vasto, *Jeune Afrique*, 385 (1968); personal knowledge

40 Pierre Cérésole

Paul Cérésole was President of the Swiss Federation in 1873, and the family was renowned in the somewhat military society of Switzerland. Pierre was his ninth child.

The Swiss are expected to perform annual military service. In the early years of this century, there was a Christian schoolmaster in Vaud named Jean Baudraz. He came increasingly to the sense that military service was incompatible with Christian discipleship. At first this was almost unconscious; he simply felt unable to read the Bible during his military service. The outbreak of the First World War compelled him to look consciously at his beliefs. He took off his gunbelt and gun and put them down before the officer in charge, saying, "I can wear these no longer." The captain gave him till the next hour struck to pick them up or face arrest. Baudraz stood firm and was arrested. At first he was sent to an asylum as crazy. But he was not crazy. He was put on court-martial, and sentenced to imprisonment.

The president of the court was Pierre's cousin Arnold, then a major. He returned home and at lunch told the company, which included Pierre, of this strange episode. The account of Baudraz began to prey on Pierre, and he came to see that Baudraz was right. He was later to describe him as "the man who in Switzerland showed us the way."

Pierre made his own stand that, as a Christian, he could not take part in war. He too went to prison. But he was not an obscure schoolteacher, but the son of a former President. There was a sensation in Switzerland.

Meantime, as he meditated in prison, Pierre conceived the idea of a peace army, to fight not other men, but the enemies which had tyrannized over mankind, hunger, need, natural disasters and war. So was born *Service Civil*, once known as International Voluntary Service for Peace, itself with great achievements, and the forerunner of other similar organizations. He began with an international work-camp to rehabilitate the villages destroyed by the war around Verdun. The volunteers lived simply and worked

63

hard at their "pick-and-shovel peacemaking". Each summer they went to the areas of greatest need, the Rhondda Valley during the depression, Bihar after the earthquake of 1934, Spain during the Civil War. Pierre worked with Gandhi in his ashram, and with the American Friends Service Committee. He campaigned to have peacework recognized in Switzerland as alternative to military service, but without success.

Then came the Second World War. Pierre, always a bridge-builder, made his way into Germany without a passport, an offence for which he was imprisoned. In January 1945 he wrote from prison: "We cannot live without the splendid values which the Army has monopolized. We must recover this treasure of sacrifice and service, and the only way to do this is the way of the cross." But prison was too much for him. A serious heart condition developed, and he died on 24 October.

Romain Rolland said: "Pierre Cérésole is the highest conscience of Switzerland. It is such conscience that saves humanity."

Source: Daniel Anets, *Pierre Cérésole, Passionate Peacemaker*

41 Sadhu Sundar Singh

Sundar Singh was one of the most remarkable people of this century. As an adolescent he despaired of life. He took a Bible and burned it to ashes. He resolved on suicide unless enlightenment came. As he sat alone in his room he felt himself flooded with light. He felt the presence of Jesus Christ.

His family tried to poison him. No-one accepted him. He found a temporary home with a Christian missionary. He resolved to be a Christian *Sadhu*, living a life of dedicated poverty, sharing his inner peace with others, singing hymns as he went.

He cared for others. He went high into the Himalayas to bring light to the peasants there. Once he found a man collapsed by the way-side in a blizzard. Sundar seemed frail, but he was very strong. He took the man on his back to the nearest village. His effort was in vain; the man had died. There is a special providence in that it is probable that having the man's body against his in the blizzard saved his own life.

Sundar was fearless, and his tranquillity could communicate itself to creatures of all sorts. A story which seems authentic tells how he was staying in a village where there was a dangerous leopard on the prowl. The Sadhu went outside to sit in meditation. His host, an Indian Christian, glanced through the window and saw him sitting there in total stillness, saw too the leopard creeping towards him. As he watched horror-struck, the Sadhu turned, held out his hand and stroked the leopard's head. Afterwards he said "Why should the leopard harm me? I am not his enemy. And anyway, as long as I trust in Christ I have no reason to fear."

As with animals, so with men. Once when he was expounding the gospel of peace a man hit him cruelly on the face so that blood flowed down. Sundar rose without a word, found water, washed his face, and came back singing a hymn. His assailant stayed to listen, shed his hostility and asked to accompany the Sadhu.

On another occasion, he was attacked by bandits who intended to kill him. Something in his face checked the death-blow as it was about to fall. "Come into our cave and speak with us," said the leader. Inside he pointed to a row of skulls. "Do you see those skulls? They are my sins. What can I do?" The Sadhu told him. The murderer became a Christian.

In the end Sadhu Sundar Singh went up into the Himalayas, and was not heard of again.

Source: C. F. Andrews, *Sadhu Sundar Singh*

42 Carie

Carie was the wife of an American missionary in China. It was a season of severe drought; the young crops withered and died. The people began to murmur: the gods were angry because of the foreigners; there had never been foreigners before and there had never been such a drought. Attendance at the little Christian chapel dwindled and fell away to nothing.

In August Carie's husband Andrew was away up country. Carie heard voices muttering outside her window. "To-night at midnight we will force the gates and kill them and throw their bodies before the gods so that rain may come."

She sent their Chinese servant Wang Amah out into the streets to find what was being planned. Wang Amah came back with the news that Carie and the children were to be murdered that night.

Carie put the children to bed early, and sat quietly. Towards midnight she told Wang Amah to prepare tea. She set out cakes and plates and cups. Then she went to the front gate and flung it open. A crowd of men shrank back into the darkness. She did not seem to see them. She went back into the house, woke and dressed the children and gave them toys to play with.

The noises outside the house increased. Carie went to the door and called, "Will you come in, please?" The courtyard was full of men with sticks and knives. They were taken aback. "Come in, friends, neighbours," she repeated. "I have tea prepared." Carie poured a cup of tea and offered it to the leader. Not knowing what to do, he took it. "Will you come in and drink tea for yourselves?" she said. "And sit down also. I am sorry my humble house has not enough seats, but you are welcome to what I have." She spoke a word of reassurance to the children.

The mob edged into the room. She caught a voice. "Strange, she is not afraid" and she replied, "Why should I fear my neighbours?"

One of them tried the organ. She showed him how to make sounds, and then slipped into the seat and sang in Chinese "Jesus, I love Your Name."

There was silence. Then one said, "There is nothing here— only this woman and these children." "I am going home," said another, and did so. Others followed. The leader looked at the children. The little boy seized his finger and pulled at it. The man was delighted and called out, "Here's a game one!" All those who had remained followed.

That night Carie was awakened by the sound of rain.

Source: Pearl Buck, *The Exile*

43 Dorothy Day

Dorothy Day was a Catholic, and up to 1932 a moderately conventional, static Catholic. Not wholly. She met Rayna Simons at the University of Illinois, and Rayna led her into radical circles. She helped to edit *The Masses*; she went to jail; she was a screen-writer in Hollywood. But she had no overriding purpose when she became a Catholic.

She tried to recover the ardour of her youth. In 1932 she went to Washington to cover a hunger march. She started questioning herself. "Is there no choice but that between Communism and industrial capitalism? Is Christianity so old that it has become stale, and is Communism the brave new torch that is setting the world afire?"

She went to pray, that somehow the talents she had might be used for the poor. When she returned to her apartment in New York she found a shabby stinking stranger named Peter Maurin. She fed him, and sent him packing. He returned. He kept returning. He haunted her. "No matter what it was that I had to do, housework, shopping, ironing, mending, cooking, Peter followed me around, not only interpreting daily events in the light of history, but also urging a program of action."

Suddenly she realized that this was the answer to her prayer. Peter's programme was not communism or capitalism, but Christian personalism, worker solidarity and agrarian distribution. By May Dorothy published the first issue of *The Catholic Worker*. By September the circulation was 20,000, and a Workers School was opening. So came works of mercy in the period of desperate poverty—food kitchens for the hungry, houses of hospitality for the homeless, country communes, retreats and peace conferences, a revived sense in the Church of the importance of the laity and of identification with the poor, and an uncompromising witness for peace which ultimately led to the US bishops' Pastoral Letter of 1983.

Dorothy Day was not an easy person. Her personal relationships were not always soundly based. She had an abortion; made an attempt at suicide; bore an illegitimate daughter. She could be dictatorial, resentful, unsympathetic, pettily angry, difficult, inconsistent.

Yet it is the testimony of those who knew her that she was a saint—not as a woolly, overstated tribute to her supposed perfection, but as a vocation, almost a good job description. Garry Wills wrote of her: "What is a saint's job? To be in all circumstances so focused on the divine presence and activity that the world gets lit through from the other side by the intensity of her gaze at and beyond her surroundings. It is a thankless job, since real saints scare people—who try to 'tame' them by reducing them to 'saintliness'. Saintliness is, in that sense, private and irrelevant. Being a saint is the ultimate challenge to others, as God's prophets realize when the divine press gang comes round... What, then, did she accomplish? Nothing but what the saint always does and must. She bore witness; she brought the message; she came from God."

Sources: Eileen Egan *Dorothy Day and the Permanent Revolution*; W. D. Miller *A Harsh and Dreadful Love*; *Catholic Worker*; *IFOR Journal*

44 Bruder Paulus

Max Josef Metzger was a Roman Catholic Priest, who was instrumental in forming a new Order, *The World Peace League of the White Cross*, later *The Society of Christ the King*, in which he was Bruder Paulus, Brother Paul. From the first World War the voice of Bruder Paulus was raised for peace. In 1917 he published a pamphlet *Peace on Earth*. From 1920, he was constantly involved in the International Fellowship of Reconciliation. At the Hague in 1928, he said, "War owes its existence to the father of lies. War is itself a lie... Thus saith the Lord, O peoples of Europe, the choice is before you, war or peace!... War is the kingdom of Satan: Peace, the kingdom of God. The 'just war' of which the moralists wrote in former days is now no longer possible... War today is a crime... We need to organize peace as men have organized war... Men of all peoples and nations, unite against this inhuman thing and declare that you will have no part in it, neither by taking up arms nor by transplanting war material nor in any other way."

When the Nazis came to power, such views were unpalatable, but he continued to proclaim them, though feeling that as a priest it was not his calling to engage in political organization. He was arrested in 1934, again in 1938, again in 1939, but each time there was no evidence against him.

When the war came he set about working for peace. He tried to get a memorandum out of the country to the Archbishop of Uppsala. The woman to whom he entrusted it was an agent of the Gestapo. Bruder Paulus was arrested on 29 June 1943. His trial was a mockery. He had hoped to use it as an occasion for witness. But, as with his Master, silence was the most powerful witness. He was condemned to death, and executed on 17 April 1944. But his letters from prison were a witness to his faith and courage. His poems were a witness. His behaviour was a witness, to his fellow-prisoners, to the chaplain (who said that he came to give consolation and received it instead), to a prison employee who recalled (not unlike the centurion at the Cross) "Never have I seen a man die like that."

Such witness is not lost. Gordon Zahn has observed how the vision of Bruder Paulus had fruition in the papacy of John XXIII and in Vatican II.

Sources: Lilian Stevenson, *Max Josef Metzger*;
G. C. Zahn, *War, Conscience and Dissent*

45 Wilhelm Mensching

Wilhelm Mensching was a missionary in Africa at the time of the First World War. He was arrested by the British, his family were roughly handled, and he was sent off to internment in India. He harboured resentment, bitterness, hatred. Two things saved him. One was the words of an English doctor: "Don't be afraid, brother. I'm a doctor. I'm not going to hurt you. I only want to help you. This war is a terrible thing. If only all men could be brothers." The other was the nonviolent campaigns of Mahatma Gandhi.

After the war he went as pastor to Petzen where he stayed for the rest of his working life. When the Nazis came to power and insisted on the greeting "Heil Hitler," Mensching continued to say "Guten tag." When an army officer upbraided him at length for this, he remembered his father's words that barking dogs would sooner or later tire and stop barking. Like Dr. Johnson he withdrew his attention, but thought, not of Tom Thumb, but of God.

One of the leading local Nazis, a man with a deplorable record of aggressive behaviour, boasted that he would have Mensching flung out of the church. Wilhelm went straight to the Nazi and told him that his work lay among the poor, that he served all God's children, and that he would not fly the Nazi flag because his allegiance was to Christ. If the man wished to denounce him he had all the evidence he needed. The Nazi was silent, and then shook him by the hand.

During the war, the Gestapo summoned the Mayor of Petzen. Was Mensching interested in war secrets? "No." Was he in touch with friends overseas? "Probably. But all he wants is to do away with war. He would never betray us. He would never spy on us. He just wants to be friends with all people." "Would you stake your life that this man would not betray us?" "Yes."

A young innocent woman was killed by an allied bomb. The Nazis wanted to use the occasion for propaganda. What would Mensching say at the funeral? Mensching minced no words. He took up this single tragedy into the common tragedy of war and the sufferings of thousands all over the world. He held them all together in "the Presence of our Common Father." Afterwards he was told that if he had swerved from his stand for humanity, he would have lost his support in the town.

At one election he and his supporters knew that their ballot-papers were marked, so that they could be identified. Courageously they asked for fresh ones. They voted "Nein." There were no reprisals.

Throughout the war, he kept at the foot of his bed the names of the leaders of the states opposed to Germany: Churchill and Roosevelt and Stalin. He would awake and remember the words "Love your enemies," and pray for international understanding.

Wilhelm once said: "When a man does evil, he's in darkness. He can't see. When I come home at night and my house is in darkness, do I seize brushes and brooms to drive the darkness away? No, I just light a candle."

Source: George Hogle in Allan Hunter *Courage in Both Hands*;
personal knowledge.

46 Lilje at the Dance

Lilje was a German railwayman who was sent by the Nazis
into Russia as stationmaster of a small town near Smolensk.
His predecessor had been harsh and tyrannical, and there had
been several attempts to assassinate him.

Lilje said to his Russian workers: "I shall give you a certain
amount of work every day, and when you have finished it, you
may go home." At first they did not believe him. Then they
found that he was a man of his word, humane and just.

One day an old Russian peasant invited Lilje to accompany
him to a wedding party in a remote village. Lilje was happy to
accept the invitation and went wearing his German uniform. As
they arrived at the village the old man said to him: "Now, for
your own safety, and that of us all, it would be better for you
to give that pistol and dagger of yours to me. I shall lock them
up till tomorrow, and while you are dancing, you will not need
them." After a momentary hesitation Lilje agreed.

He had a wonderful evening with fun and dancing. In the
morning the old peasant returned his weapons, and drove him
to the station.

"I will tell you," he said, "why I thought it better you
should not have your weapons. All those young men who were
dancing in the same room with you are Partisans, sworn to kill
any German soldiers they can lay hands on. Among them, you
were safer unarmed."

"But," said Lilje, "I *am* a German soldier. Why did they
not kill me as they were sworn to do?"

"Oh no," replied the old man. "You are not a German
soldier. You are a reasonable man who treats Russian workers
kindly. That is known all over the country here; no-one has
anything against a man like you."

Source: Heinz Kraschutski in A. Ruth Fry
Victories without Violence

75

47 Otto Schimek

Otton Schimek was born in Vienna in 1925. He belonged to a poor family; his father was a locksmith, his mother had been in domestic service. He was the thirteenth child, but several of the others died of malnutrition.

In 1942, at the age of seventeen, he was conscripted into the army. He was a reluctant soldier, but was not yet ready to make a stand on principle. But he refused to take part in looting, and this of itself led him into disfavour.

The Nazis had taken civilian hostages from among the Poles. Otto Schimek was offered a pardon for his failure to cooperate in looting on condition that he shot the hostages. He refused, saying "I am a soldier but also a Christian. As a soldier I fight the enemy but not the innocent people of this country. I will not obey the order." He had not gone the whole way with the New Testament in saying 'No' to war, but he had taken seriously the moral obligations of the Christian faith, and the traditional doctrine of the Just War, far more seriously than most, who have allowed their actions to be dragged down by circumstances.

Otto Schimek was charged with "cowardice in the face of the enemy," a charge which was wholly false. He was shot on 14 November 1944. He was only nineteen.

Appeals for mercy were disregarded, except that he was buried in consecrated ground at Machowa near Cracow. His grave is now a place of pilgrimage for Poles and Austrians. One of his fellow countrymen has said "His example should shine forth not only in Poland but also beyond its boundaries."

Source: Peggy Attlee in *Just Peace* March 1984

48 Franz Jägerstätter, Austrian Martyr

Franz Jägerstätter was a very ordinary extraordinary man, peasant farmer and martyr. He was born in Austria in 1907, and married in 1936. His life was uneventful. Almost all that is known about him is that he was an exceptionally devout Catholic. In 1938, the Nazis annexed Austria. There was a plebiscite to ratify the annexation. Cardinal Innitzer endorsed his. Franz's priest, critical of the Nazis, advised him to vote Yes. Franz Jägerstätter deliberately spoiled his ballot-paper.

In the years that followed, he supported the poor and needy with generosity, but he refused any contributions which might benefit the Nazi state, and he refused to claim a bonus from the Nazis for the birth of his three daughters. As a farmer he was undoubtedly helping the Nazi food-production programme, but he could hardly do otherwise: this was an inescapable part of his involvement in society. In general his opposition was unrelenting.

He was required to report for military training in 1940 and 1941. On both occasions he went; on both he felt tainted and stained; on both he secured release to return to his farming. He made it clear that he would not go a third time. To friends he said "I may never co-operate in an unjust war. God will provide for my wife and children."

The third summons came in February 1943. His bishop reasoned with him, found him unyielding, "and declared that he would be permitted to take this path only if he were certain he had been called to it through some exceptional inspiration from above and not from some private decision of his own". Franz saw this as confirmation of his resolve.

He was arrested, and on 6 June 1943 condemned to death for undermining the military power. The prison chaplain pleaded with him, but he insisted that he could not take part in an unjust war. Only then did the chaplain tell him of the execution of Father Reinisch for refusing the military oath of allegiance. Franz's eyes lit up, as if he were shedding a load. He said, "I have always been sure that I could not be on the false path. If, therefore, a priest came to this same decision and died for it, I can, too." He was beheaded on 9 August 1943.

He seems to have been the only Austrian layman to make such a stand. He wrote of the Christian struggle: "We bring no pistols or arms to our war, but, rather spiritual weapons—before all else prayer." He added: "Let us love our enemies, bless those who curse us, pray for those who persecute us. For love will emerge victorious and will last for all eternity—and happy are they who live and die in God's love." In the tiny graveyard of St. Radegund lie the ashes of the peasant who defied the European dictator. His story is an inspiration to others.

Source: G. C. Zahn *Solitary Witness* (1965)

49 Elizabeth Pilenko: Mother Maria

Elizabeth Pilenko was born of a well-to-do Russian family, and had an excellent education. She became a teacher and was influential locally. Then came the war and the 1917 revolution. Elizabeth was instrumental in saving victims of the Terror. She was by now Mayor of her home town, and worked hard for peace between Communist and non-Communist. She was put on trial and acquitted. Unable to help more, she escaped to Paris and started a new life as a member of a religious order under the name of Mother Maria. She served the down-and-outs in the filthy hovels along the banks of the Seine. She helped Russian refugees. She took over a chateau and turned it into a home for those who had come to give up hope. When, in 1940, the Germans occupied Paris, she hid Jews within her hospital.

The Gestapo caught up with her. She was arrested and taken off to a concentration camp in Poland. There she ministered to her fellow prisoners. Even the guards called her "That wonderful Russian nun." There was a new building in the camp. The authorities called it a bath-house. In reality it was a death-chamber.

A group of the women were selected to march into this building. They knew they would never come back. Elizabeth was not one of them. But as they stood in the queue one of them, a young girl, broke into hysterics. Elizabeth walked over to her and said: "Don't be frightened. Look! I'll take your turn." So Elizabeth Pilenko passed to her death.

It was Good Friday 1945.

Source: *Christian News-Letter*, 17 April 1946

50 Bill Brough

There cannot be many pacifists who have represented their university at boxing. Bill Brough is one of them.

He grew up in Northumberland, a Methodist, at a time when the voices of Henry Carter and Donald Soper, as Kenneth Greet later, were strong and prophetic. Loyalty to Jesus Christ for him meant refusal to take part in war, even against systems as evil as the Nazi or the Imperial Japanese.

So when war came, Bill stood as a conscientious objector, and, like hundreds of others, went to face unarmed the same dangers as the soldiers, to save life not to take it, in the Friends' Ambulance Unit. Bill went to serve in the fighting with the Japanese in Asia.

While he was there, he experienced a change of heart and mind. He came to feel that he could not be separate from those who were using military means to combat aggression. He volunteered for the army. In the sector where he was serving the only army he could join was the American army. He won the highest award for valour that the Americans give to non-citizens—and came out a pacifist.

As he looked back on his experiences he testified that he not merely felt safer without the protection of arms: he was safer. While in the FAU he had been walking unarmed through the jungle with a fellow-worker. Suddenly, without warning, a Japanese soldier slipped out of the jungle with rifle at the ready, eyed them, and equally silently slipped back again. If they had been armed they would have been shot down without a moment's hesitation.

Bill Brough is now a psychiatrist and a professor, helping to heal the causes of violence in the human mind.

Source: Personal knowledge.

51 Fei-Yen

Fei-Yen was a Chinese girl of the labouring classes, but exceptionally bright. She learned to read and write, then began to teach others.

Then the Japanese came. Fei-Yen was vulnerable, as was any young girl. The invaders would seek to rape her. Her father would be honour bound to protect her. He would be killed; the family would be left destitute. Fei-Yen must "think out a plan for herself." Her father meant that she should take her own life. But Fei-Yen was a Christian.

She thought out a plan for herself. She left home and went to help in a medical clinic fifteen miles away. Her help there was greatly valued. But before long, the Japanese reached the neighbourhood of the clinic. The doctors had to give Fei-Yen the same advice with the same meaning.

She went away, persuaded a farmer to give her some men's clothes and boots, cut her hair, and returned to the clinic as a coolie. Next day she was helping to look after wounded Japanese soldiers at gun-point. At nightfall the Japanese retired to the safety of their own camp. All night Fei-Yen and the doctors nursed Chinese guerrillas, all day they cared for Japanese wounded.

Fei-Yen heard that the Japanese had destroyed her village and killed her brothers and sisters. It did not make her hate or alter her care.

She went fifteen miles through the Japanese lines to fetch needed medicine from a hospital. None of the others had the courage to go.

Some months later, after the missionaries had been withdrawn, a doctor visited the area of the clinic. He found there a well-organized refugee camp. Only the missionaries were empowered to set up such a camp. But there were no missionaries. It was all Fei-Yen's work. "I said I was working for the missionaries who couldn't speak Japanese. And they still think there's a missionary somewhere about, but, you see, I take all the messages."

The bell went for evening prayers. Fei-Yen led them. She prayed for God's protection for the friends and relatives of them all. "And please bless the Japanese people at home in their own country who must be suffering just as we are from this war." She ended: "O God, please help us to root out of our hearts all hate and pride and fear and anger because we know they are the things that makes wars like this possible. For Christ's sake. Amen."

Source: The doctor to Muriel Lester in
Allan Hunter, *Courage in Both Hands*

52 Mitsuo Fushida, Margaret Covel, Jacob Deshazer

Captain Mitsuo Fushida of the Japanese airforce was a man of sterling courage and a ruthless patriot. He was commander of one of the squadrons which bombed Pearl Harbour in 1941. In the subsequent fighting, he had three narrow escapes from death: once when he was blown off an aircraft carrier with two broken legs but was picked up by a destroyer; once when he crash-landed in the sea to be rescued by a junk; once when he was shot down in Borneo and escaped through terrible privation in the jungle.

After the war, he heard from an old friend who had been a prisoner-of-war in an American camp how an eighteen-year-old girl named Margaret Covel had ministered to her "enemies". He learned too that both her parents, Christian missionaries, had been executed by the Japanese as spies. At first the girl had been filled with hatred. Then she realized that her parents would have been asking God's mercy for their killers. Her attitude must be the same. Fuchida could not understand this. Then he read a pamphlet by Sergeant Jacob DeShazer *I was a Prisoner of Japan*. Here was an American airman who as a prisoner of war had been brutally treated by the Japanese for over three years. He had blazed with anger and resentment and hatred. But memories of Sunday School began to burgeon within him. There was a different way, power of a different sort. DeShazer gave himself to that way and that power. He went back to Japan to share his insight with his former enemies.

Fuchida was puzzled and fascinated. He asked for a Bible. He read and read, and was still puzzled. Then he came on the passage where Jesus on the cross cries "Father, forgive them; they do not know what they are doing."

So Captain Fuchida renounced the way of violence and war, and gave himself to the Christ who is our peace.

Source: Mutsuo Fuchida, *My Testimony from Pearl Harbour to Calvary*

53 Jean Goss and the Sadist

Jean Goss was born in 1920, and the outbreak of war saw him in the French army. In 1940 he experienced a profound revelation of the reality of Christ, which transformed his life. Shortly after, he became a prisoner of war. His experience of Christ led him to realize that Christ's love knew no boundaries or limits and was the mainspring of all his actions. We are limited by our weakness, but must set no bounds on our love if we would follow him.

In the camp there was a sadistic SS guard. When the French prisoners came in, wearied from their day's work, he would take one of them on one side and beat him unmercifully for the sheer pleasure of causing pain. This was too much for Jean. One evening as they were lined up, he stepped out of line, marched up to this guard, and said "Since you like beating people up, beat me up today." "What makes you think I wouldn't, Frenchy?" said the man threateningly. "Your conscience." "Conscience. What conscience? I haven't got a conscience." "Oh, yes, you have," said Jean. "If you hadn't got a conscience you'd have hit me already. You haven't—and I don't think you're going to." With that he turned his back on the tormentor and stepped again into line. When he turned round this tough ruthless sadist was crying. He never beat up a prisoner again.

Jean came into contact with men like Henri Roser, and women like Anne Boirard. Through them he learned about the work of Gandhi. Since then he and his Austrian wife Hildegard have travelled the world with the gospel of nonviolent love, challenging the Second Vatican Council, and building up cells of nonviolent revolution in Latin America.

Source: Personal Knowledge.

54 Bayard Rustin

Bayard Rustin was a Black American with a rich personality and a golden voice who as quite a young man was on the staff of the Fellowship of Reconciliation. He was one of those of whom John Oman might have been referring when he said, "When I say a Christian I mean one with whom to see is to act."

Bayard had a light tenor voice of high quality. He sang both Negro spirituals and Elizabethan songs with great sensitivity. More than once he calmed angry passions by the power of music.

Bayard was one of those who set themselves to break segregation in the southern states of the USA, so he deliberately sat in the section of a bus reserved for whites only by traditional practice. The bus driver telephoned ahead, and at the next town four tough policemen dragged Bayard out, kicking and beating him. Bayard put his arms out in the form of a cross and said gently "There's no need to beat me. I am not resisting you." At this point three white Southerners intervened to check the police. When a policeman turned on one of them, Bayard, still very gently, said that there was no need to intervene. An elderly white promised to follow them to Nashville and see that justice was not abused.

In the car the policemen abused him verbally. He looked them straight in the eye. They dropped their gaze.

At Nashville the police captain said, "Come here, Nigger." Bayard walked up to him. "What can I do for you?" "Nigger, you're supposed to be scared when you come in here." "I am fortified by truth, justice and Christ; there is no need for me to fear." The captain was flabbergasted. Eventually he exploded, "I believe the Nigger's crazy."

After a time Bayard was taken to the District Attorney's office. The elderly white was there watching. The DA questioned the police and Bayard closely, and in the end said "You may go, Mr. Rustin."

On another occasion, Bayard went into a small Midwestern restaurant. The waitress ignored him. He went up to her. "I would like to have a hamburger." "I'm sorry, but we can't serve... er... you... coloured people here."

Bayard went up to the superintendent. She explained first that coloured people were dirty and idle, and second that other people would walk out. Bayard took her through facts till only prejudice was left. He asked her to try an experiment. He would sit conspicuously for ten minutes in the front of the restaurant. If anyone left, he would go; if no-one left, she would serve him. No-one left. She brought his hamburger and said, "What will you have to drink with it?"

Bayard was addressing a meeting once when there was a scuffle at the back. He instantly stopped speaking, and went where the peace-making was needed. A Christian is one with whom to see is to act.

Source: International Fellowship of Reconciliation; personal knowledge.

55 Betty Elliott

Five missionaries from the United States plunged among the fierce Aucas in the jungles of Ecuador. On January 6, 1956 they were visited by two women and a man, whom they welcomed warmly. On January 8 they were killed by the suspicious Indians.

Betty Elliott was left widowed with a small daughter Valerie. Did God call her to continue her work among the gentler Quichuas? To return to the US? Or was there some other call?

She began to learn the Auca language, to learn about the people. She went up in one of the mission planes and flew low over the Auca settlements. She saw a man whose photograph she had found among her husband's effects. She dropped him a food parcel. He raised his arms as if in "a pleading gesture and smiled and shouted." Not long after, the Aucas raided and looted the house of an English missionary.

Betty heard of two Auca women in a Quichua settlement. As she walked through the jungle to find them both she and her guides had a sixth sense that the Auca people were watching with suspicious and murderous hostility from behind the jungle screen. She reached the settlement and met the women with a strange sensation of déjà vu. Then she realized that her husband had photographed one of them two days before his death. She broke through the women's fear and made friends.

Betty now brought little Valerie to join her in the Quichua settlement. That very day the Aucas murdered a Quichua, leaving eighteen spears in his body, and abducted his wife. But the Auca women showed sorrow. The friendship with Mankanu and Mintaka developed. So did Betty's Auca, though her pronunciation of their names never seemed quite right. They came with her to the missionary settlement. Quichua who had never seen one of the murderous Aucas exclaimed with surprise "Why, they've two legs like us!" She took them by plane to the nearest town for dental treatment. They saw donkeys for the first time.

Now, three years after her husband's murder, she went—in two senses—to the heart of the Aucas. Mankamu and Mintaka preceded her. With her went little Valerie, the sister of one of the other murdered men, ten Auca women and boys, half a dozen Quichua Christians. They were greeted by one of her husband's murderers. Yet he did not seem hostile, and was soon treating Valerie as his own daughter. Betty and Valerie slept among them in hammocks such as the Aucas used, ate the same food, followed the same life-style, played the same games.

There was a moving moment before they went to sleep on the first night when Fermin, one of the Quichua Christians, prayed "Our much beloved Father, you have brought us safely to this place. Here we are with our new friends. We say thank you very much. We love them, we prayed much for them. Show us how to live together like brothers. Open their hearts, plant your word in them like seeds which will grow." The Aucas did not understand the words, but the spirit was infectious.

Before Betty and Valerie had been many months among them those who massacred the missionaries were saying "We did not do well to kill them." A few months later they were asking "Do we ever do well to kill?"

So out of death came life, through a woman and a child who thought nothing of revenge or of the justice under which revenge masquerades, who walked with courage through the gates of death, and replaced the spiral of violence with the spiral of love.

Source: E. Elliott, *A Bridge in Green Hell*

56 Will Warren

Will Warren was a Quaker who felt called to go in 1971 to strife-torn Northern Ireland. He would describe himself as "a simple, ignorant, and rude old man"—simple enough to believe that Jesus thought very strongly that good is stronger than evil, and that if you return ill for ill and violence for violence, you double the amount of ill or violence, and that there is something of God in everybody.

He went to Ireland in concern for those who were suffering, whether Catholic or Protestant. He mingled with all. Then one day he came home to find ten armoured cars and fifty soldiers waiting. All guns were pointed at him. The door was broken down, his possessions all over the place. He was taken to the "barracks" (police station) and interrogated for four hours. He answered questions about himself—but not about others. In the end they let him go. On his return some members of the Provisional IRA were waiting for him. They told him where he'd been, who had interrogated him, the questions they asked, and the answers he gave, and didn't give. And they knew they could trust him. When some of the youngsters, sick of killing, wanted to settle back into civilian life, they turned to him.

It was more difficult to win the confidence of the Protestants, but he achieved that too.

Two Protestants were murdered. Retaliation on retaliation seemed likely. Will went to the Protestant Paramilitaries and the Catholic Provisionals and persuaded them to meet. He said "Look here. If I forget about my pacifism, and you forget about your Republicanism, and you about your loyalism, let's see where we go from there." He went on. "If a Protestant murders a Catholic, I will agree to a Protestant murdering the Protestant murderer. If a Catholic murders a Protestant, I will agree to a Catholic murdering the Catholic murderer. You'll get the pleasure of killing people without sectarian murder." After a stunned silence they agreed. A little after he called them again: "That seems all right. But instead of killing them, why not just

kneecap them?'' To shoot through the kneecap disables only.
So he gradually got the penalty reduced from permanent disablement to temporary disablement, and nearly persuaded them to
accept dye on the hands instead.

Will Warren was a maverick. Few would have used that
technique. But his courage, his integrity, his *love* won the
confidence of both sides, and during his time in Ireland he
on his own greatly reduced the violence.

Source: Reconciliation Quarterly, December 1980;
personal knowledge

57 Dom Helder Camara

Two priests in Latin America identified themselves with the poor in such a way that they became world famous, but they chose different roads. Camilo Torres came from Colombia. He spoke of his call: "I was chosen by Christ to be eternally a priest, moved by the desire to give myself full-time to love my neighbours." He thought the traditional order of Catholic priorities should be reversed so as to become: love, the teaching of doctrine, liturgical worship. Love for him meant feeding the hungry, clothing the naked, care for the sick and imprisoned. That meant changing the structures of society which every day create and multiply these conditions. So he said, "I am a revolutionary because I am a priest," and, "Revolutionary action is a priestly struggle." Elections did not change the order of society. Strikes brought out oppression. "The people know that only armed rebellion is left," said Camilo. So he himself became a guerrilla, and was ambushed and killed on 15 February 1966.

Helder Camara, later Archbishop of Recife, would accept most of Camilo's analysis and commitment. But his commitment is to nonviolent revolution as Camilo's was to violent revolution. Dom Helder's pilgrimage has been a strange one, out of right wing fascist militancy into education, which gave him an insight into the true nature of Brazilian society. He was challenged to look at the shanty towns. At first he felt the problem without getting involved in the struggle. But he became more involved as "a pastor who is there and sees his people suffer". The hierarchy sent him off to the remote and depressed area of the North-East, no doubt in part to shut him up. This they have signally failed to do.

Helder Camara is a Christ-centred man: "I really believe in Christ; for me Christ is not an abstraction; he is a personal friend." He is a pacifist because he has given himself to Christ, and is dedicated to righting wrongs without intensifying the wrongs by committing them himself. He has claimed kinship with Martin Luther King. He sometimes speaks of "peaceful violence". He believes that Christianity means change here and now: "I am trying to send men to heaven, not sheep. And certainly not sheep with their stomachs empty and their testicles crushed."He can sympathize with those who take the way of violent resistance, and has been known to describe armed revolt as "legitimate but impossible in Latin America". It is not certain that he means by "legitimate" more than "in accordance with the Law, whether the Old Testament or the Church's doctrine of the Just War," for he does not see it as falling within the fullness of Christ. It is legitimate because provoked, impossible because it would be squashed. He sometimes claims not to hold a religious position here, but this is a paradox. He is assailing neutrality: "I detest anyone who remains unperturbed, or silent, and I love only those who fight, who dare to do something."

Some have tried to play down Dom Helder's nonviolence, wrongly. In 1965, he was speaking of the need "to stimulate a nonviolent action as an arm of peace in the underdeveloped countries". What was needed was not guerrilla action but "a profound and radical change which presupposes divine grace and a transformation of public opinion which can and must be aided by the Church of Latin America and of the entire world". Real grassroots education, effective "conscientization", is the alternative to violent change. His personal vocation, he has said, is to be a pilgrim of peace, the foundation of his stand the Beatitudes. "The option for Christians is clear. We, as Christians, are on the side of nonviolence, and this is in no way an option for weakness and passivity. Opting for nonviolence means to believe more strongly in the power of truth, justice, and love than in the power of wars, weapons and hatred." Dom Helder's stand is love-centred, Christ-centred. Among the Brazilian bishops, he began Moral Pressure for Liberation, which changed its name to Action, Justice and Peace, revolution without violence and against violence in the establishment. The governments were using the M-bomb, the weapon of misery. Action, Justice and Peace was not seeking to stifle the "No" of the oppressed but to help it to be courageous and positive, beautiful, and constructive. It was no "dull and dismal movement, tolerated and tolerating".

God rejects the dull and tepid. Helder Camara is an activist. He knows that real change may not come quickly. He knows that violent change is self-defeating. he knows therefore that active nonviolence must keep peace and must not flag, and must arise from commitment.

Those in power sent an assassin to murder him. The killer marched up to the Archbishop's humble house and banged at the door. A little man opened it and blinked at him: "Yes?" "I want to see Dom Helder Camara." "Oh yes. Do come in and sit down. I am Dom Helder. What can I do for you?" The gunman was already out of his depth. "You are Dom Helder? I have come to assassinate you." Dom Helder smiled. "Here I am. Assassinate me, I am ready to go to God at any time." The murderer blurted out "You are with him already," and rushed from the house.

There are three reasons for nonviolence. First, the oppressors hold the big guns. Second, the oppressed must be aware of their dignity as children of God; in violence they lose that dignity. Third, and above all, because it is the way of Christ.

Violence escalates. The spiral of violence must be replaced by the spiral of love.

Dom Helder, his house machine-gunned, his life threatened, his friends tortured and murdered, has lived that active pursuit of justice through nonviolent love.

Sources: Helder Camara, *Spiral of Violence*;
J. de Broucker, *Dom Helder Camara*;
Mary Hall, *The Impossible Dream*;
J. M. Bonino, *Revolutionary Theology Comes of Age*

58 Fanny Lou Hamer

Fanny Lou Hamer grew up in the cotton fields of the Mississippi delta, among the poorest of the poor, the youngest of a family of twenty. Slavery may have been abolished in the previous century; you would scarcely have known it. Toilets at petrol stations seemed to recognize three sexes "Men" "Women" and "Colored". Segregation, apartheid, was the rule. Power was kept from the Blacks by the inadequacy of their schooling combined with complex literacy tests.

Fanny Lou grew up and married. Unable to have children of their own, she and her husband adopted two. As she worked in the fields, and her back became tired, she would ask, "Can't we change all this?"

In August 1962 at a Christian rally, she found it was her right to vote. She went to register, failed the literacy test, and told them she would be back every month. In January 1963 she was registered. Meantime, her attempt to exercise her constitutional right, and to encourage others to do so, had lost her her job. She was already a marked woman. She had, to sustain her and others, a radiant faith, and a radiant voice. Often her hymn singing defused tensions and fears. She became Field Secretary of the Student Nonviolent Co-ordinating Committee. She was harassed by the Mississippi authorities, the Ku Klux Klan, the White Citizens' Council, the FBI. Her telephone was tapped. Her life was threatened. She never sank to hatred or violence.

Not long after she had become a full-time SNCC worker, Fanny Lou Hamer was arrested with others for sitting at a "Whites Only" lunch counter. In prison she was brutally beaten, suffered kidney damage and impaired eyesight. The policemen were never punished. She said, "It wouldn't solve any problem for me to hate whites just because they hate me. Oh there's so much hate, only God has kept the Negro sane."

So now she sang and she preached and she organized. She was active in the Mississippi Freedom Democratic Party, when the Democratic Party failed them. She opposed the

Vietnam War. She attacked a system in which leaders are more interested in profits and power for the rich than help for the poor. She helped to organize Martin Luther King's Poor People's Campaign. She was instrumental in getting the Head Start programme into Mississippi, and the poorer children feel the impact of this still.

They called her a prophet. She was fearless and selfless. She was always Christian: "Christianity is being concerned about your fellow men, not building a million-dollar church while people are starving right around the corner. Christ was a revolutionary person, out there where it was happening. That's what God is all about, and that's where I get my strength." The others called her their "emotional rock". She sang her way into their hearts. She changed the words of one song from "Go tell it on the mountain, that Jesus Christ is a-born" to "Go tell it on the mountain to let my people go." For to her they were the same. Where Jesus Christ is, there is good news for the poor and deliverance to the oppressed. And she was always nonviolent. The good news was not that violence can be overcome by violence but that violence can be overcome by suffering.

In the 1970s to the effects of polio as a child, of kidney and eye trouble, of diabetes and heart trouble, was added breast cancer. She died on 14 March 1977. A service in Ruleville Junior High Auditorium was packed with mourners. The Mississippi State Legislature passed a resolution in her honour sponsored by four black congressmen, who would not have been there except for her. On her simple tomb are words which she made her own: "I am sick and tired of being sick and tired."

Source: *Sojourners Magazine*, December 1982.

59 Sarah Corson

Sarah Corson is a citizen of the USA, who had come to Latin America with her husband and four children at the request of a group of villagers to help them establish a church, a fish hatchery, and other projects to meet basic human needs. From there they moved on, but were asked to return. By now her husband was committed elsewhere. Sarah came, leading a team of seventeen young folk including her sixteen-year-old daughter Kathy and fifteen-year-old son Tommy. They were far in the jungle, two hundred miles from the nearest city.

There had been an election, followed by a military coup. Sarah knew that the soldiers were blaming the Americans for resisting their coup, and were threatening a massacre. But she thought they were far from the scene of action, and anyway not involved in local politics.

Nightfall had come. The moon was shining tranquilly over the fish ponds they had helped to build. Suddenly she became aware that thirty soldiers, rifles out, were rushing the house. She froze with fear, and in a split second prayed "God, if I have to die, take care of my family. And God, please take away this fear. I don't want to die afraid. Please help me to die trusting you." She was suddenly aware of God's presence. She raised her voice: "Welcome, brother. Come in. You do not need guns to visit us... You're all welcome. Everyone is welcome in our house."

They pushed her roughly in, herded the team into the kitchen, ransacked the house for arms. The leader abused her for trying to stop their revolution. She protested that she had come for self-help projects and to teach the Bible. He did not know the Bible. She spoke of God's love, and the need for humans to love one another. He glared at the words "Jesus teaches love your enemies." "That's humanly impossible." "That's true, sir. It's humanly impossible, but with God's help it is possible." "I don't believe it." "You can prove it. You came here to kill us. Kill me slowly now. You will see that you cannot make me hate you. I will die praying for you, because God loves you and we love you too."

The soldiers marched them down a trail towards a lorry. Then the commander said "Halt! Take the men only." He escorted the women back, saying that he had never before disobeyed an order, and he might pay for it with his life. But he knew what they did to women prisoners. "I could have fought any amount of guns you might have had. But there is something here I cannot understand. I cannot fight it." The men were taken away. Some were tortured, but they were eventually released, though that lay in the future.

Should they hold their usual service on Sunday? They thought they would pray at home. But then they had a message from the commander. He wanted to come to their service. He came with a bodyguard. The whole church welcomed them as they always welcomed visitors. "Brother," said one, "we don't like what you did to our village but this is the house of God, and God loves you, so you are welcome here." The soldiers were dumbfounded. They could not understand what was happening. The commander asked to enter the pulpit. He said that he had not believed it to be possible for Christians to love their enemies. He now saw that it was true. He had never believed in God, but if what he had experienced retained its strength he would never cease to believe. "I don't know God, but I hope some day I shall, and that some day we can once again greet each other as brothers and sisters, as we have done this morning."

He went back to lunch with Sarah, on fish from the fishponds. His parting words were: "I have fought many battles and killed many people. It was nothing to me. It was just my job to exterminate them. But I never knew them personally. This is the first time I ever knew my enemy face to face, and I believe that if we knew each other, our guns would not be necessary."

Source: *Sojourners Magazine* April 1983.

PART IV: CORPORATE ACTIONS

60 William Penn and the Pennsylvania Quakers

William Penn, born on 14 October, 1644, under the shadow of civil war, was to become a servant of the Prince of Peace. His father was an Admiral, honoured for his fighting against the Dutch, broken by failure in the West Indies. But these grave happenings turned the young boy to God.

The family moved to Ireland. There came the Quaker Thomas Loe, a man of charm and courage. The Admiral would not judge him without hearing him. His witness to the Inward Light touched young William's memory of his earlier experience.

The Restoration of the monarchy saw the restoration of the Admiral. Young William went to Oxford, but his anti-clerical views led to his expulsion. He continued his studies in France, where the Huguenot Moîse Amyraut taught something near to Quakerism. He returned to England and was still close to his military father. But in 1667 in Ireland he heard Thomas Loe again, and this time gave himself fully to the Quaker faith, though he retained some aristocracy and militancy. Estranged now from his father, he turned to Friends, and fell in love with Gulielma Springett whom he married in 1672. But before that he was pleading for liberty of conscience, and went to prison in the Tower for it, and wrote his great book *No Cross, No Crown*. His father came to admire his courage and his principles, and on his death-bed commended the son to the King and Duke of York.

So it came about that William Penn received from the King the grant of a tract of land in America almost the size of England. On his arrival, Penn would have nothing to do with the violence and exploitation which besmirched so many of the relations between settlers and Indians. He established his territory as a Holy Experiment, and entered into a treaty of peace with the Indians, "the only league between those nations and the Christians which was never sworn to and never broken," said Voltaire. It provided that "all Christians and all Indians should be brothers, as the children of one Father, joined together with one heart, one hand, and one body.'' The frontier was secure; no drop of Indian blood was shed by a Quaker; no drop of Quaker blood by an Indian; traders moved in safety; Indians would take care of the children of the Quakers while the parents were at Meeting to worship.

For seventy years this continued, till the war party and the Church party at home ousted the Quakers from their control of the colony. Violence from the whites encouraged the Indians to violence. Even so, the Quakers remained largely untouched. Thomas Chalkley in the eighteenth century recorded three deaths only, two of men who had discarded their principles and taken up arms, and one woman whose mind had become beclouded with fear.

Source: Mabel Brailsford, *William Penn*

61 Ferenc Deak and Hungarian Independence (19th century)

In the mid-nineteenth century, Hungary was oppressed by Austria. In the year of revolutions, 1848, Kossuth rose with violence and was repressed with violence. This is the background to what is perhaps Christopher Fry's most powerful play *The Dark is Light Enough*.

Fry wrote the play in the knowledge that nonviolence had in fact succeeded where violence had failed. Deak, a Catholic landowner, after the Kossuth débacle, called the nation to nonviolent resistance. They were not to acquiesce in the oppression: "Your laws are violated, yet your mouths remain closed. Woe to the nation which raises no protest when its rights are outraged! It contributes to its own slavery by its silence. The nation which submits to injustice and oppression without protest is doomed." But the protest must be nonviolent. "This is the safe ground on which, unarmed ourselves, we can hold our own against armed force. If suffering must be necessary, suffer with dignity."

Deak drafted a plan for Hungarian independence in education, agriculture and industry. The plan involved a boycott of Austrian goods and systematic non-cooperation with the Austrian government. At the same time he insisted that nonviolence of action should be accompanied by nonviolence of attitude. There was to be no abusive language, no lack of courtesy, just non- cooperation. The Austrian tax collectors came, and the Hungarians refused to pay. The Austrian authorities distrained their goods and put them up to auction, but no Hungarian auctioneer would participate in their sale. The Austrians imported auctioneers from Austria, but no-one bid for the distrained goods. So the Austrian government had to import buyers from Austria. But by now the cost of disposing of the property was greater than the original exaction.

The Austrians billeted soldiers on Hungarian homes. The Hungarians did not refuse or resist; they simply ignored the soldiers and did nothing for them, sending them, as the English expression goes, to Coventry. It was the soldiers who called on their government to stop billeting them on unwilling hosts.

The Austrians declared the boycott of Austrian goods illegal. Deak had called for the protest to be within the law, but an unjust law could not be obeyed. The Hungarians continued the boycott. The prisons were full, and the cost of maintaining the prisoners far exceeded any benefit Austria might hope to gain.

Meantime the Hungarians refused to take up their seats in the Imperial Parliament.

The Emperor Franz Josef changed his tack. He attempted conciliation. He offered a sop, a partial grant of Hungarian requests. But Deak and the Hungarians were adamant. They stuck out for their full claims of independence. Franz Josef called Deak to him. "Deak, what should I do?" he asked, surely one of the strangest questions directed by an autocratic ruler to a rebellious subject. "Give Hungary her liberty, Your Majesty," said Deak.

Franz Josef was not persuaded. He imposed military conscription. The Hungarians refused to obey the order. The outside pressures on the Empire were building up. Franz Josef was desperate. In the end he gave up, and on 1 Feb 1867 inaugurated a new constitution.

Source: R. B. Gregg, *The Power of Non-Violence*;
A. Griffith, *The Resurrection of Hungary: A Parallel for Ireland*;
A. J. P. Taylor, *The Habsburg Monarchy 1808 – 1891*

62 The People of Monterey

One of the stranger historical episodes of the second half of the nineteenth century happened in 1875. News reached the Emperor of China that the Chinese working on the railways in California were being exploited and maltreated. He resolved to teach the United States a lesson, and sent seven heavily armed junks to attack Monterey. The Emperor, swathed in his own cocoon, had no idea of the width of the Pacific, and miscalculated the provisions needed. The sailors were saved from death through thirst only by a sudden rainstorm, in which they lowered the sails and used them as canvas troughs. Eventually they succeeded in reaching Monterey. Fifty gunners stood to their cannon ready to blast out any resistance. There was no resistance. On the contrary the whole town came down to welcome the visitors and to offer them hospitality. The Emperor's soldiers renounced their allegiance, and settled in California either as railway workers or as fishermen.

Source: R. Halliburton, *Story of His Life's Adventures*

63 Queen Lydia Vatea and her people (19th century)

The centre of Christian work in Fiji was Viwa; the converts included the Queen, Lydia Vatea. But many were not converted, and, under a member of the royal house named Thakombau, were coming in armed force to annihilate the Christians. The Christians remained firm. They were prepared for martyrdom, saying, "Heaven is very near." They went as usual outside the village to pray. Yet, curiously, they were praying not for deliverance, but for the souls of their enemies, and at the same time lifting up their voices in joy and praise.

Meantime the Queen went to Thakombau, and dropped to her knees. But she did not ask him to spare the Christians; she asked him to join them. She spoke of her joy in her faith, and of his need.

The army grew in strength, equipped with firearms and clubs. So far from resisting, the Queen and her fellow-Christians had food prepared for their persecutors and welcomed them. They were God's people, and were confident that they were in His hands. As their oppressors grew in number, so their oppressors' purpose shrank and weakened. Towards evening they said, "We came to kill these people, and we cannot lift a hand," and began to withdraw. As they made for their canoes, the Christians, mindful of Jesus's words about going the second mile, helped them with their burdens including the very weapons brought for the intended massacre.

Source: O. S. Rowe, *Life of John Hunt*

64 Te Whiti and the Maoris (19th century)

Te Whiti was a Maori, known as the Prophet of Parihaka. He had heard the Christian Gospel from Lutheran missionaries. He understood it better than the British soldiers who, complete with chaplains, over-ran New Zealand and stole the Maoris' land.

It was in the 1870s. The settlers—it is noticeable that a white man going to live overseas is a settler, a black or coloured man coming to Britain is an immigrant—wanted pasture land. They began to build roads through the territory of Parihaka and to sow grass on the soil. Te Whiti met them firmly but without violence. The young men of the village built fences across the roads and ploughed up the soil. His followers were arrested; so was Te Whiti. But he had taught his message well. An army of 2500, led by cavalry, advanced on the village. They were met, not by armed warriors, but by children with skipping-ropes, who skipped in the path of the cavalry, and refused to move even though the horses were almost upon them. Eventually an army raid destroyed the village.

So Te Whiti failed. Or did he? The settlers conquered. Violence, greed and injustice seemed to win—did for the moment win. One greater than Te Whiti said, "They have their reward." But there are guilty consciences now, a century later; and the Maoris are recovering pride in their own history. The spirit of Te Whiti, the same spirit which guided Mahatma Gandhi and Martin Luther King, lives today.

Source: *Now*, Nov. 1982

65 Rondon and the Chavantes

In the early years of this century there was a remarkable soldier in Brazil named Candedo Rondon.

For three hundred years, there had been war between the Europeans who had settled in Brazil and the indigenous American Indians. You can still see a river where a company of settlers were massacred by Indians: it is called *Rio des Mortes*— the river of death. So fighting went on and on and on. Rondon was blooded in these wars—literally, for he was grievously wounded. But he recovered, and as Colonel and later General was put in command of the Brazilian army in the war with the Indians.

Rondon was a soldier, and sometimes—not always—soldiers, who are men of action, see further than politicians or, I fear, churchmen. Rondon saw that, for three hundred years, war had got nowhere. He was a Christian, a mystic, and a man of constructive vision. He reformed his army and renamed them "The Indian Protective Service". He gave them, I suppose, the most extraordinary command ever given to an army: "Die if you must, but never kill." Die if you must, but never kill.

His troops moved in among the Indians bringing help. Some lost their lives: not a single Indian life was lost. Gradually the Indians were won over. But the fiercest tribe, the Chavantes, refused. Rondon sent in twenty-five picked men. They were massacred. Not one tried to retaliate. There was a nationwide demand for reprisals. Rondon refused. He sent in twenty-five more under his disciple Vanique. They met hostility patiently. Then they saw an Indian army marching on their camp: "It's our turn now," they thought. But the army had blunted spears. They had come to sign a treaty of peace with the White Indians.

So peace did what war had failed to do. Not without cost. Those first twenty-five were martyrs for peace. that is Christ's way—the way of the cross—to conquer by suffering, not by inflicting suffering on others however savage, cruel and violent those others may be.

Peace hath her victories no less renowned than war.

Source: J. Ferguson, *The Politics of Love*

66 Sir Hubert Murray

Sir Hubert Murray was a remarkable proconsul, widely loved and respected. He was a fine scholar, boxer, oarsman and swordsman. After a surprisingly unsuccessful career as a barrister, and a short period in the army, he joined the administration in what was then British New Guinea, and rapidly rose to the top. At a time when colonial policy often punished a whole village for the crime of one man, he arrested individuals only and then treated them constructively. At the beginning of his thirty years as Governor of Papua, raids by one village on another were frequent. Murray's practice was to go first to the injured village and find out who were the attackers. If he could not find out, he would go himself into the wilds, disregarding arrows fired at him. When fired upon, he would sit down and smoke. He would leave presents to attract the people and bring them to talk. When the raiders were found he did not punish them, but took them with him on his tours of inspection, finally enrolling them as constables. He would whimsically say that murder was the favourite crime of the Papuan, a high-spirited adventure or even a social duty. One Papuan, learning he might be punished for the murder of a girl, remarked, "But there are plenty of girls left!" So for most of his career there was no prison in Papua; he simply led people from a social ethos which permitted or encouraged violence to one which outlawed it. Soldier as he was, he knew that you do not encourage people to act without violence by repressing or punishing violence violently. In 1923 the League of Nations said, astonishingly, "Papua leads the world in justice, wisdom, mercy, and the efficacy of her rule." In 1937 the people of Papua praised his impartiality and his loving and constructive concern for their welfare, and hoped that (though he was now over seventy-five) he would stay on as their Governor. When he died, an elder named Ahuia Ove spoke of his friendship, impartiality and understanding of their ways: "Who is like him in Papua?"

Source: *Manchester Guardian*, 16 June 1936;
Pacific Islands Monthly, 15 May 1940; J. G. Latham in *DNB*

67 Russia 1905 – 6

Pre-Revolutionary Russia was governed by autocratic Tsars who claimed a divine right to rule, backed by the nobility and in general by the Church.

In the early years of this century, dissatisfaction was growing, among the peasants and the intelligentsia alike, who were calling for representative government.

In January 1905, on "Bloody Sunday", a large crowd joined in a peaceful march to the winter palace outside St. Petersburg to present a petition. They were unarmed. They were met by an armed guard who opened fire on them. When the fusillade had finished a hundred lay dead, and three hundred more were wounded.

This sparked off action in protest throughout the country. Many of the poor who had believed in the Tsar's fatherly concern for them were now alienated from him. Sixteen members of the Academy of Sciences wrote a declaration calling for a change of government; it was signed by 326 professors, and eventually by 1200 leading scholars. Lawyers refused to appear in the courts of a tyrannical régime. The Manufacturers' Association voted aid to the victims' families. Army officers involved in the action were excluded from clubs. Nearly 500 liberal intellectuals wrote to the Officers of the Russian army, telling them not to take arms against the unarmed. Factory workers went on strike. The railways were dislocated. Whole provinces broke away and declared their independence. Newspapers ignored censorship.

By October the country was paralysed. The Tsar put out the October Manifesto, permitting an elected legislature. The concession, though significant, was limited. The disturbances continued.

But in December 1905 the Bolsheviks and Mensheviks joined to turn this largely nonviolent protest into a violent uprising. It was crushed equally violently. The nonviolent revolution came to an end because it had turned to violence. This is not just the judgement of those committed to nonviolence. It was the judgement of Lenin.

Something had been achieved. A great power had been shaken: concessions had been made.

Sources: S. Harcave, *First Blood: The Russian Revolution of 1905* (1964); S. M. Schwarz *The Russian Revolution of 1905*, ET 1967

68 Gandhi

All nonviolent work today is indebted to Gandhi. He in turn was indebted to ancient Indian traditions of *ahimsa* (non-harming), to Jesus and the New Testament, to Thoreau "On the Duty of Civil Disobedience", to Tolstoy *The Kingdom of God is within You*, and (for the positive stress on creative work) to Ruskin *Unto This Last*.

Gandhi's great principle was *satyagraha*, truth-force, or, as some prefer, truth-influence; he himself liked to call it "soul-force". Truth is all powerful and needs no force of arms. *Satyagraha* is a total pattern of living, comprising love, truth, openness and nonviolence. It involves the readiness to suffer, not too inflict suffering:

> If blood be shed, let it be our blood. Cultivate the quiet courage of dying without killing. For man lives freely only by his readiness to die, if need be, at the hands of his brother, never by killing him. No power on earth can stand before the march of peaceful, determined and God-fearing people. Nonviolence is more powerful than the mightiest weapon of destruction devised by the ingenuity of man.

Out of many acts in which he shared we pick out seven.

Transvaal

He went as a lawyer to South Africa, and there quickly felt the weight of racial prejudice; they called him the "coolie barrister". There were thousands of Indians labouring in South Africa. In 1906 the Transvaal government tried to introduce an oppressive system of legislation. Under Gandhi's influence the leading Indians refused to register, and were sent to prison. The Prime Minister, Smuts, agreed to repeal the legislation if the Indians would register voluntarily. They agreed, and he broke his word.

Gandhi now organised a major demonstration, a nonviolent march from Natal to Transvaal. Characteristically, he notified the government in advance. Gandhi was in and out of prison. The 4000 marchers were all arrested and taken back to Natal. They remained nonviolent.

Now world opinion, especially from the Government of India, began to harden against Smuts. He saved face by appointing a Committee and releasing Gandhi, but he was not prepared to have Indians on the Committee. At this moment the European railway workers went on strike. Gandhi, again characteristically, called off all Indian action until the strike was settled. The sympathy this won far outweighed any political advantage he might have gained by exploiting the government's difficulties.

The strike ended, and Smuts was constrained by public opinion to give way. The Indians secured the abolition of registration and of the poll-tax, the validation of their marriages and an assurance of justice under the laws. This was Gandhi's first great victory without violence.

Champaran

Gandhi returned to India in 1914. At Champaran in the North the peasants were exploited by the planters, being compelled among other things to plant 15% of their land with indigo. In 1917 Gandhi went to investigate. The planters protested; the magistrate ruled that he should leave. Gandhi replied courteously that he was there out of duty and to ascertain facts. If the law punished him, he would accept the penalty but not neglect his duty.

He then went on recording statements from the peasants, and ensured that there were others to carry on. He was arrested and pleaded guilty, setting up a conflict of duty in the magistrate—obedience to the law or humanitarian action. The magistrate was nonplussed. The governor intervened, and set up a Commission of Inquiry including Gandhi. The Commission found for the peasants against the planters, and their exactions were terminated.

This was a nonviolent struggle for economic justice.

Khaira

In Western India, in Khaira, the crops failed. Gandhi went to see. He found 600 villages close to starvation. The people could not pay their taxes. Gandhi told them of their rights; when the crops failed they did not have to pay taxes they could not afford. But the government exactions continued. Now there was a mass movement of *satyagrahis*; their property might be taken, and their persons beaten or imprisoned, but they would not pay taxes and they would not use violence.

In the end the government gave way. If the better-off farmers paid, the poor would be exempt.

It should be recalled that this action took place against a background of war.

Non-cooperation

In 1921-2 Gandhi began a campaign of non-cooperation directed against British rule in India. Part of the campaign involved the injunction to the Indians to spin, and to bring their foreign cloth to be burned. Part was directed against oppressive actions such as the Amritsar massacre and legislation such as the Rowlatt Acts. The main tactic was the refusal to pay taxes. Gandhi of course warned the government. But he insisted on nonviolence, and when a mob in Chauri Chaura burned some policemen to death, he called off the whole campaign. He himself was arrested. He spoke of the massacre, the public floggings, the orders to crawl down a street. India was not allowed arms: how could she respond except by non-cooperation? He was guilty and asked for the maximum sentence. He received six years' imprisonment, and responded, "Your Honour, I wish to thank you. I could not have expected greater courtesy."

This might seem a failure. India was not at the time liberated. Yet the withdrawal from an action which was uncontrolled was in the end a far more important witness to *satyagraha*.

Vykom

In the South, in the village of Vykom in Travancore, the main road ran by a Brahman temple. The Brahmans would not allow outcastes, known variously as "untouchables", Harijans, Dalits, to use the road.

Some young leaders consulted Gandhi who advised them from afar. They began by taking "untouchables" with them into the forbidden territory. They were beaten up, offering no retaliation, and arrested. Volunteers began to pour in to take their place. The police barred the road. The protesters stood facing them in prayer They organized themselves into six-hour shifts. Gandhi insisted that they must continue until the hearts of the Brahmans were changed. Weeks passed and months. The rains came. The low-lying ground where the confrontation stood was swamped. The police cordon took to boats. The protesters continued to stand though the water reached their shoulders. After sixteen months, in the autumn of 1925, the Brahmans said, "We cannot any longer resist the prayers that have been made to us, and we are ready to receive the untouchables." The road was opened to all.

This local action affected caste reform throughout India. It is one of the most moving of all acts governed by non-violent love.

The Salt March

The other great imaginative act of Gandhi in seeking freedom for India was the Salt March. The British government exercised a monopoly on salt, making it, selling it and taxing it. He wrote to the Viceroy calling for a change in taxation; otherwise they would break the salt laws.

On 17 March, 1930 he gathered with seventy-eight of his followers and began a pilgrimage to the sea 241 miles away. He was sixty-one. The March took twenty-four days, and, as they passed, the seventy-eight grew to thousands. On 16 April, he rose at 5 a.m. in a village by the sea, walked into the water with an earthenware bowl, scooped out the seawater, brought it to land and boiled it, till only the deposit of salt was left. He had broken the law.

Now all along the coasts Indians did the same. In the first week there were sixty-nine arrests. Gandhi was left for a month. Then they sent three officers with pistols and thirty policemen with rifles to arrest him!

113

The Salt March united the peoples of India. All over, *satyagrahis* witnessed and suffered. Of these, 90,000 were arrested, men, women and children. Eventually the Viceroy, Lord Irwin (later Lord Halifax) talked with Gandhi, and the campaign was called off pending a Round Table conference in London.

The Final Act

In August 1947, through years of patient *satyagraha* India had her freedom. But now Hindus fled from Moslems and Moslems from Hindus. For five days Gandhi fasted. He was seventy-six and near to death. They came to him, Hindus and Moslems: "Gandhi, here are our clubs, our swords; we will leave them with you to prove that we do not intend to use them again. Please end your fast." But some cried, "Let Gandhi die!" He recovered, only to be shot by a Hindu fanatic. He died with the words "Hai Ram!" "Oh God!"

A million people gathered for his funeral.

He brought India her independence, and the world the knowledge that active nonviolence, springing from religious conviction, was also practical politics.

Sources:
M. K. Gandhi, *The Story of My Experiments with Truth*;
L. Fischer, *The Life of Mahatma Gandhi*;
C. O. Peare, *Mahatma Gandhi: Father of Nonviolence*;
R. B. Gregg, *The Power of Nonviolence*;
Joan V. Bondurant, *Conquest of Violence*

69 Berlin 1920

After the armistice of 1918, the Weimar Republic was faced with enormous difficulties of economic and social unrest.

On March 10, President Ebert was presented with an ultimatum by Lieutenant-General von Lüttwitz, in alliance with Dr. Wolfgang Kapp, and with the backing of Ludendorff and other leading army officers whose sympathies were monarchist and right-wing. The government rejected the ultimatum, and warned that they would use a general strike to counter a coup d'état. It is one of the most remarkable governmental declarations of history. They did not want a civil war. They suspected anyway that the army would not fight against the *putsch*.

On March 12, Kapp and his supporters began their march on Berlin. The police sided with them. Ebert abandoned Berlin, refusing or unable to use counter-violence, and left for Dresden and Stuttgart; the city was occupied next day. Kapp and von Lüttwitz declared the formation of a new government.

By Saturday evening in Berlin, the Independent Socialists had rallied. It is reckoned that they had available enough men and weapons to overpower the usurpers. But they wanted to avoid a civil war. Instead they called a general strike from the Sunday night, agreeing that there was to be no provocation, that all was to be done in friendliness and good humour, and that they would fraternize with the soldiers.

The fraternization began on Sunday morning. The streets were packed with civilians buzzing friendlily around the soldiers. The generals sent cavalry to drive them off, but they simply moved from one group of soldiers to another.

Ebert was firm. The states were directed to refuse to co-operate with the usurpers, and work with the legitimate government. A call for a general strike was issued by the Social and Democratic Party members of Ebert's government: "There is but one means to prevent the return of Wilhelm II: the paralysis of all economic life. Not a hand must stir, not a worker give aid to the military dictatorship. General Strike all along the line." The strike was

115

widely supported by political and religious groups, though the communists were slow to come in. The civil servants joined the strike. The new government had no support from the ministries—and no money.

By March 15, they were making proposals for a compromise. The Ebert government rejected them. The general strike was now fully operative. The only service to be maintained was the food supply. Traffic was at a standstill. Gas and electricity were cut off. Some of the army leaders went back to the legitimate authority. An aeroplane dropped leaflets over Berlin declaring "The Collapse of the Military Dictatorship". The dictators began to panic and to shoot strikers. The strikers remained firm. On March 17 the Berlin Security Police demanded Kapp's resignation.

Kapp escaped to Sweden. Von Lüttwitz resigned. The Brigades of the dictators were ordered to march out of the capital. The people lined the boulevards on either side and stood in silent vigil as the troops marched away. Some troops could not resist firing at the crowd. The crowd remained silent. Not a voice was heard until the sound of tramping feet had died away.

Said the historian Erich Eyck, "Since the regular tools of the state had been found wanting, only immediate intervention by the populace could have saved it so soon." A military historian, Lt-Col D. J. Goodspeed, wrote, "To all intents and purposes the coup seemed to have succeeded. Yet it was broken, very largely because the people would not obey the new government."

Sources:
D. J. Goodspeed *The Conspirators*;
E. Eyck *A History of the Weimar Republic*;
W. H. Crook *The General Strike*;
G. Sharp *The Politics of Nonviolent Action*;
eye-witness account by Wilfred Wellock in A. Ruth Fry
Victories Without Violence

70 The Ruhrkampf

In 1923, three years after the successful nonviolent resistance to the abortive Kapp *putsch*, the German people were faced with another campaign in face of French and Belgian occupation of the Ruhr. This was a campaign of non-co-operation and it was backed by a wide range of people, industrialists and trades unionists, civil servants and ordinary citizens. The campaign was, however, accompanied by some sabotage. Exponents of nonviolence have usually avoided violence against things as well as against people, partly because it is difficult to sabotage things without at least endangering human lives, and partly from a deep-rooted feeling that once you embark on violence it may not be easy to stop, and that to be nonviolent you have to take a commitment to nonviolence, though half a century later Nelson Mandela was to make a powerful plea of his refusal to use violence against people while being driven to a more demonstratively violent resistance to the instruments and resources of apartheid.

The *Ruhrkampf* is often treated as a failure. It was not a failure, though it cannot be regarded as a total success for nonviolent methods. But the French found that they lost effective control of the Ruhr, and that their attempt to divert its resources into their own exchequer was proving unprofitable: economically the losses outweighed the gains. Their immediate response to the passive resistance campaign was violent repression. This cost them the support of world public opinion and public opinion in France itself, and led to the fall of the government. The new government negotiated with the Germans and agreed to evacuate the Ruhr if the passive resistance were brought to an end. Though there were complicating factors (there always are) it can be seen in broad historical terms that the campaign achieved the end of freedom from an oppressive and exploitative alien power.

Sources:
Adam Roberts (ed.), *Civilian Resistance as a National Defence*;
E. Eyck, *A History of the Weimar Republic*;
G. Sharp, *The Politics of Nonviolent Action*

71 Abdul Ghaffar Khan

Abdul Ghaffar Khan was a Pathan, a member of a Moslem people with a proud tradition of military courage and the bloodfeud. As he lay in a British prison he read the Holy Qur'an and came to the belief that the Prophet's strength lay in his patience and willingness to suffer. This accorded with Gandhi's proclamation of *satyagraha*. It led him to the formation of the *Khudai Khidmatgar* or Servants of God.

Abdul Ghaffar Khan, himself a chieftain's son, was a very different man from Gandhi. Louis Fischer wrote: "As Gandhi was of the soil and sand of India, Ghaffar Khan is of its rocks and crags and raging torrent. The hot blood of sharpshooting, trigger-happy mountaineers courses in his veins but he has adopted the philosophy of complete non-violence and so have thousands of brother Pathans." He was a huge man of strong personality. He sought social and educational reform. In 1926, he came to the conclusion that this needed a political party; in 1929 he organized the Khudai Khidmatgar to be its direct action wing. The membership pledge was exacting:

1. I put forward my name in truth and honesty to become a sincere Khudai Khidmatgar.
2. I will sacrifice my wealth, life, and comfort for the liberty of my nation and people.
3. I will never be a party to factions, hatred, or jealousies with my people; and will side with the oppressed against the oppressor.
4. I will not become a member of any other rival organization; I will not stand in any army.
5. I will faithfully obey all legitimate orders of my officers all the time.
6. I will live in accordance with the principles of nonviolence.
7. I will serve all humanity equally. The chief objects of my life shall be attainment of complete independence and religious freedom.
8. I will at all times observe truth and purity in all my actions.
9. I will never desire any reward whatever for my service.
10. All my efforts shall be to please God, and not for any show or gain.

The Servants of God were organized in strict military discipline, but carried no weapons, not even a staff. It is notable that the

Congress Party (unlike Gandhi) was secular and saw nonviolence as a tactic only. But the Servants of God saw nonviolence as a religious commitment. By 1938, the numbers had risen from 500 to over 100,000. They included women.

The movement met with astonishing success. Anyone who broke the pledge of nonviolence was instantly dismissed. The Congress flag they flew bore the crescent of Islam in place of the spinning-wheel. The red shirts they wore, as well as their striking appearance, made them conspicuous. They used all the established techniques of processions, voluntary closure of businesses, slogans (including "Allah Akbar!") and songs, the suffering of shooting, beating and imprisonment without murmuring, or retaliation. For one period of nine days they actually took over control of the city of Peshawar, controlling traffic, patrolling the streets, and organising normal life. In other areas they persuaded the landholders to refuse payment of revenue to the government but organized their own revenue and administrative service.

Some Moslems denounced the Servants of God for undermining the military spirit of Islam by preaching nonviolence. Abdul Ghaffar Khan responded by citing the Holy Qur'an to the effect that Peace was the coping-stone of Islam, and pointing to the forbearance and self-restraint of some of the great figures of Moslem history, as well as showing the courage with which the Pathans faced the rifles of the government troops. Sometimes they were shot, but soldiers of a Garwhal regiment refused to fire on unarmed, disciplined, nonviolent demonstrators, and a British civil servant commented that their defection "sent a shock through India, of apprehension to some, of exultation to others." The Turkish woman journalist Halidé Edib was deeply impressed by the Servants of God. This was a new interpretation of force, she wrote: "Nonviolence is the only form of force which can have a lasting effect on the life of society and man. And this, coming from strong and fearless men, is worthy of study." Gandhi came up to the North-West only in 1938 and was deeply impressed by what he found. When an official from Southern India said that there was no meeting-ground between the people of the North and South, Gandhi answered that nonviolence was the golden bridge.

119

The achievement of the Servants of God was the reversal of the attitudes and practices of centuries; the substitution of cooperation and constructive action for partisan violence; the turning of military discipline from the infliction of suffering on others to a willingness to suffer in a good cause; the acclimatization of nonviolence within Islam in accordance with the highest traditions of that great creed.

After the partition of India, the government of Pakistan tried to force the Pathans into their military state. Abdul Ghaffar Khan had spent fifteen years in British prisons for nonviolent resistance to British militarism; he and his companions had no more truck with Pakistani militarism. They faced the government with the same courage. He, his family and his leading associates were clapped into prison again, where he spent a further fifteen years mainly in solitary confinement. Eventually, in 1964, at the age of seventy-four, he was released to go to London for medical treatment. In 1965 he was granted asylum in Afghanistan. There, ten years later, Ved Mehta met him, still rugged and powerful, still clothed in the characteristic dark red shirt. He told of the influence of education in a Christian mission school upon him, how his effort to improve the condition of the Pathans led him to prison, how there he read the Holy Qur'an and was deeply moved by the patience, suffering and dedication of the Prophet Muhammad, and how Gandhi's ideas of nonviolence and his Constructive Programme brought him to a new vision and commitment which he accepted and proclaimed in the name of Allah. But India had forsaken Gandhi, as, centuries before, it forsook the Buddha. The Pathans were faithful. Gandhi had once said to him, "Nonviolence is the child not of the cowardly but of the brave. A Pathan is brave, so nonviolence is natural to him."

It is a moving thought that the Russians in Afghanistan may have been met in some parts with disciplined nonviolence.

Sources: Joan V. Bondurant, *Conquest of Violence* (1965); R. R. Diwakar, *Satyagraha: Its Technique and History* (1946); E. Easwaran, *A Man to Match his Mountains* (1984); L. Fischer, *The Life of Mahatma Gandhi* (1951); Ved Mehta, *Mahatma Gandhi and his Apostles* (1977); Pyarelal *A Pilgrimage of Peace* (1950)

72 Melville Mackenzie and the troubles in Liberia

In 1932 Liberia was hit by civil strife. Houses were burned, crops destroyed, people killed. The Government of Liberia appealed to the League of Nations, which appointed Dr Melville Mackenzie, a member of the Secretariat, as mediator. He worked closely with a representative of the Government.

He was quick to sum up the situation, and realized that the overt cause of the troubles was dispute over tribal boundaries, but that the real cause lay simply in the fact that the tribes were armed, and that very fact made them fearful and suspicious of one another.

Dr Mackenzie insisted that the fighting stop and that the tribes surrender their arms before any act of arbitration could take place. This took two months, but he achieved it. When this was accomplished, he was able to adjudicate on the frontiers. There was such relief at the end of the deaths and destruction, that one village which had been destroyed was rebuilt by the very people who destroyed it as part of their contribution to the peace.

Source: *Peace-Making in Africa*

73 The Butte Copper workers

Butte, Montana, was effectively controlled by a Copper Mining Company which under-paid and intimidated its workforce in such a way as to provoke violent reactions and to intensify its own violence. In 1934, a bitter strike broke out. The Governor intervened. He made no attempt to prevent or discourage the strikers from their purpose. His object was to avoid bloodshed. he arranged with the Sheriff that picketing would be authorized provided that it were peaceful. The Company imported armed gunmen, but they found no pretext for using them. There was no violence, no bloodshed, no fighting, no damage to property, no lives lost, in marked contrast with all previous labour disputes. There was not even any call for extra policing. After four and a half months the Company negotiated higher rates of pay!

Source: *The Christian Century*, 17 October 1934

74 The Danish Resistance to the Nazis

On 9 April 1940, the Germans invaded Denmark and occupied the country for five years. For the first three, apart from the outlawing of the Communist party, there was little interference with the domestic affairs of the country, and the majority of Danes chose to retain a relative security rather than challenge the invaders. The Communists began to establish a clandestine cell structure. Church groups encouraged resistance within the law, strengthened Danish national consciousness within youth groups, and even wrote publicly against the Nazis. The government kept Nazis out of office. The Civil Service used bureaucratic procedures to be unhelpful to the occupying power. Ordinary citizens boycotted German cultural events, and isolated the invaders.

By the middle of 1943, German reverses led to new hope of liberation among the Danes, and greater severity on the part of the Germans. The pinch was felt mainly among the workers; the rich were doing well enough out of war contracts. From February, strike action began. But the main wave of strikes began in August. It was a grassroots movement. The government and the trades union leaders tried to stop it, without success. The Germans demanded massive autocratic action. The government resigned.

Now the Germans were directly responsible. Up to this point the Danish Jews—or Jewish Danes—had been protected by the government. The grassroots organization set to with vigour. Of the 8,000 Jews, 7,000 were smuggled into Sweden. Only 450 were arrested. Even the Danish Nazis refused to betray the Jews. The organization, courage and dedication were alike superb. And the underground railroad, once set up, could be used for others. Over 8,000 Danes "wanted" by the Germans escaped that way. Out of 450 allied pilots shot down, 102 made their way to Sweden.

In June 1944, a tough ruthless SS Corps destroyed some of the most precious symbols of Denmark (the Tivoli Gardens and the Royal Porcelain Factory included) in retaliation for attacks on arms factories. There were executions, a curfew, a ban on meetings, and the death sentence for strikers. As a result virtually the whole of Copenhagen went on strike, meeting in the streets in defiance of ban and curfew. The uprising was largely nonviolent. German shootings killed 102 Danes, but the Germans could not cope. They sealed off the city. No use. They were forced to give way, rescind the bans, send away the SS Corps. They had no answer to nonviolence.

Illegal printing was important, for communications matter. So does humour. A German sentry was marching up and down behind a chest-high wall of sandbags. On the other side a notice was placed "He has no trousers on."

The Danish formula then was aggressive nonviolence: mass non-cooperation, humour, ostracism, humanitarian sacrifice, clandestine rescue, music, unobtrusive obstruction.

Sources: ·

J. Bennett, *British Broadcasting and the Danish Resistance Movement 1940 – 5*, Cambridge, 1966;

A. Berthetsen, *Oktober 1943* Copenhagen, nd;

A. P. Goldstein and others, *In Response to Aggression*, New York 1981;

J. Haestrup, *From Occupied to Ally* Copenhagen, 1963;

A. P. Hare and H. Blumberg, *Nonviolent Direct Action*, Washington, 1968;

E. Lund, *A Girdle of Truth*, Copenhagen, 1970

75 The Norwegian Teachers

When the Nazis occupied Norway their puppet-ruler Vidkun
Quisling tried to establish a fascist Corporative State, beginning
with the teachers. He created an organization with compul-
sory membership. There were 12,000 teachers in the country.
Over two thirds—according to some figures, over three quar-
ters—signed a refusal to take part in fascist education, saying,
"I cannot regard myself as a member of the new teachers'
organization."

The government threatened to dismiss them, and closed the
schools. They held classes in their homes. Despite censorship,
news spread. Tens of thousands of parents protested.

A thousand male teachers were arrested and sent to a concentration camp, put on starvation rations and an inhuman régime.
Nearly all stood firm. Meantime the schools reopened, but the
teachers refused to conform even when threatened that their
comrades would be killed.

Quisling visited one of the schools and completely lost his
temper, screaming, "You teachers have destroyed everything
for me!" Scared to alienate public opinion further, he eventually
released the teachers. The teachers' organization was never set
up. The schools were kept free from fascist education. In the end
it was Hitler who was forced to command Quisling to abandon
his Corporative State.

The Norwegian teachers' resistance is one of the finest
examples of nonviolent resistance to Nazi tyranny.

Source: Gene Sharp, *The Politics of Nonviolent Action*

76 The Wives of the Jews

In Germany in 1943 there were mass arrests of the Jews remaining free. They were taken to mass camps where they awaited massacre.

In Berlin those with "Aryan" relations were concentrated in a prison in the Rosenstrasse. Somehow their wives found out where they were. Six thousand women gathered outside the prison in the early morning and cried at the tops of their voices for the release of their husbands, who, despite orders to the contrary, began to appear at the prison windows. Again and again the guards set themselves to disperse the crowd; again and again they regrouped. Then, when the hours of work came round, there was at last a respite for the authorities. They must have thought the problem had gone away, but with the afternoon the crowd massed again, and the square was packed with voices crying for release.

The SS, ruthless as they were, did not bring out the machine-guns. They saw the growing crowds, and a demonstration without parallel since the Nazis achieved full power. They negotiated, and eventually released all the men.

The story is told by one of the men who survived through the courageous persistence of the women.

Source: Heinz Ullstein, *Spielplatz meines Lebens*

77 Le Chambon-Sur-Lignon

Le Chambon-sur-Lignon is an ancient Huguenot village in the Cévennes. Here in 1934 came Pastor André Trocmé, himself born of a French Huguenot father and a German mother, with his wife Magda, daughter of an Italian father and a French mother. If not quite a United Nations in themselves, they spanned Europe between them. In Le Chambon the Trocmés, with their old friend Edouard Théis, built up a small community dedicated to peace, founding a celebrated international secondary school, Le College Cévenol.

Then came the war and French reverses. A Jewish woman came to them for help. They sent her to the mayor for a ration card. The mayor said, "You're crazy; if we keep her here the whole community will be endangered; you must send her away." They did not see her again. But they rebuked themselves for carelessness and felt the guilt of her death. They resolved that never again should a Jew be turned from their doors.

France surrendered, and the subsequent occupation intensified the persecution of the Jews. André Trocmé stood up in his pulpit and said, "Our duty is to hide Jews." They set themselves to do just that. One Jewish woman was taken to a farmhouse. "Are you really a Jew?" said the farmer. "Yes," she answered nervously, waiting for the blows to fall. "Come down, come down, children," he cried. "What a privilege to welcome one of the Chosen People!"

The French police came and demanded that the Jews be given up. "I am a shepherd," said André, "not a policeman...I know no frontier to my flock. Everyone is a guest here."

The Jews were hidden in quarries and caves and mountain recesses. The police found none.

To save the Jews the community at Le Chambon had to forge ration cards, identity cards, passports, and smuggle the refugees into Switzerland. All his life, André had a bad conscience about these deceits. But, as he said, they did no-one harm, and they saved life. As a Christian he refused to have anything to do with the taking of the lives of the oppressors.

The Gestapo were tougher than the French police. They arrested twenty-three of the younger members of the community, including Daniel Trocmé, André's cousin, and shot most of them. They would raid the village unexpectedly—yet, never unexpectedly, since there was always an anonymous telephone warning.

André and Edouard Théis were arrested in 1943. There were communist guerrillas in the concentration camp. They would discuss whether Jesus Christ or Karl Marx had more to offer the human race. But the name of Karl Marx was banned. So they substituted the name of the French figure-head Philippe Pétain, and were in good odour with the guards for discussing whether Pétain was a greater man than Christ. The pastors were offered conditional release. They refused to accept any compromise. A pragmatic communist called them fools, but, when they were released shortly after unconditionally, came to see that there was something in their stance.

Later, the Gestapo took the decision to assassinate them. Two Gestapo agents came to André: "We have just been at a meeting where the assassination of you and Théis was decided upon. We advise you to disappear now." So they did, and through many adventures were kept safe.

At Le Chambon one of the leaders was the volatile doctor Le Forrestier. One of the younger members was arrested for an indiscretion. He smuggled a note out to the doctor asking for help. Le Forrestier thought he could get into Le Puy on his doctor's pass. He did so, and asked to see the German commander. He said, "We loathe what you are doing, but we do not hate you. We will do all we can to undo your work. But you're not going to drag us down to use your methods. We are Christians. We don't use violence. We don't take lives."

While he was there, there was a bank robbery. Cars were investigated. Le Forrestier's had no proper pass for Le Puy. The car was searched. Under the passenger's seat was found a revolver. It was nothing to do with the doctor. He had picked up a hitch-hiker, who was a guerrilla, and had left his gun without permission. Le Forrestier was arrested, and eventually killed.

It might be that that was all we knew. It happens that we know more. We know that the commander was deeply moved by the doctor's witness, and when the Gestapo wanted to raze the village to the ground and kill the inhabitants, he said: "No, I am in charge here, and you shall not do it. I have spoken with these people. I do not understand them, but I know that they do not belong to the guerrillas." So, through the doctor's quixotic witness, the village was spared, and the work of saving the Jews went on. Two thousand or more Jews were saved in this way.

After the liberation of France, the Trocmés showed their utter consistency in saving the lives of German oppressors and French collaborators from mob anger.

André Trocmé was the leader of the community. Trocmé was like a hurricane in action. Edouard Théis was the man who kept them stable: Magda compared him to a rock unmoved by a torrent.

Trocmé was once preaching in England: "Have love in your hearts," he said, and then, "No. Forgive me, my friends. I do not speak your English language well. I do not know what the heart is except an organ for pumping blood round the body. Have love in your lives."

Source: Personal Knowledge.
See also: P. Hallie, *Lest Innocent Blood Be Shed*

78 Guatemala 1944

General Jorge Ubico had been dictator of Guatemala since 1931. His thirteenth year was to prove unlucky for him. He was a ruthless autocrat, who succeeded in presenting a benevolent face to the outside world. He was recorded as saying, "I am like Hitler, I execute first and give trial afterwards," and again "As long as I am President, I will never permit a free press, nor free association."

With the war, Guatemala joined the allies. The war brought inescapable changes. German owners of coffee plantations had given Ubico considerable support: they were ousted. The dictator in nearby El Salvador had fallen. The presence of American troops led to the dissemination of democratic ideas. The wartime situation did not allow economic drift: employers and workers were alike dissatisfied. Students and young intellectuals were restless with hope of a new and different world.

Towards the end of May 1944, forty-five lawyers petitioned for the removal of an oppressive judge who dealt harshly with political opposition. The dictator blandly asked for the charges to be specific. To his surprise these were swiftly forthcoming; to everyone else's surprise they were allowed to be published in a newspaper.

This time of year saw an annual parade of schoolteachers and children in honour of the President. The day before, two hundred teachers petitioned for an increase in salary. Their leaders were promptly arrested and charged with conspiracy. The teachers boycotted the parade, and in requital received notice of dismissal.

On June 20 a manifesto was published, calling for social justice, an end to governmental terrorism and the right to organize opposition parties, and announcing the formation of the Social Democratic Party. Meantime there was student unrest, with demands for the release of two students from prison, the reinstatement of two dismissed lecturers, and the principle of university autonomy. Ubico's response was to declare a state of emergency and institute repressive measures. He, who had once expressed his admiration for Hitler, castigated the opposition as 'nazi-fascist''. Some students took refuge in the Mexican Embassy. But the younger professional men came out in support, and on June 23 the school-teachers went on strike.

The dictator was on record as saying that if 300 respected Guatemalans were to ask him to resign he would do so. On June 24 two men presented the *Memorial de los 311* to his office. The signatories were risking their lives. They called for the suspension of martial law and the establishment of effective constitutional guarantees. Students had a peaceful march past the US Embassy. The army and police were taken by surprise: they had been expecting riots and did not know how to deal with nonviolent demonstrators. A peaceful meeting demanded the President's resignation. But that evening the police broke up with violence a neighbourhood religious and social celebration.

On June 25 the Foreign Minister asked to meet with the two men who had delivered the memorial. At the same time there was a noisy but still peaceable demonstration outside the National Palace where the people found themselves confronted with soldiers, cavalry, tanks, armoured cars, machine-guns, and armed police with tear-gas. The two men, whose names were Carbonell and Serrano, were asked to go out and "calm the people". That afternoon women dressed in mourning went to the Church of St. Francis to pray for an end to the atrocities of the previous evening. Then they processed silently through the city. Despite their obvious peaceability the cavalry charged and fired on them. Maria Chincilla Recinos, a teacher, became the first martyr of the revolution. The government violence was counter-productive: "the mask had been torn from the Napoleonic pose, revealing Ubico and his regime standing rudely on a basis of inhumanity and terror."

Talks were broken off. There was a general strike and shutdown in which workers and employers concurred. The city was paralysed. The paralysis eventually led to a confrontation. The opposition delegates told Ubico, "Guatemala had known nothing but oppression under your rule." Ubico retorted that the people of Guatemala were not ready for democracy and needed a strong hand at the helm. The delegates were sent to sample public opinion. They returned to report the universal demand for Ubico's resignation, the lifting of martial law, freedom of the press and of association, and an end to attacks on the people. Meantime the paralysis of the capital continued.

On July 1 Ubico withdrew in favour of a triumvirate of generals. One, General Ponce, tried to establish himself as Ubico's successor, but was ousted by a general strike, student strike and coup d'état.

The action in Guatemala did not establish democracy. But it was a brilliant demonstration of the fact that even a ruthless dictator finds nonviolent protest difficult to fend off. Mario Rosenthal wrote:

> Energetic and cruel, Jorge Ubico could have put down an armed attack...He could have imposed his will on any group of disgruntled, military or civilian, and stood them up against a wall. But he was helpless against civil acts of repudiation, to which he responded with violence, until these slowly pushed him into the dead-end street where all dictatorships ultimately arrive: kill everybody who is not with you or get out...
>
> The movement that brought Waterloo to Guatemala's Napoleon was, fittingly, a peaceful, civilian action; the discipline, serenity and resignation with which it was conducted made it a model of passive resistance.

Sources:
M. Rosenthal, *Guatemala: The Story of an Emergent Latin-American Democracy* (1962);
R. M. Schneider, *Communism in Guatemala 1944–1954* (1958);
G. Sharp, *The Politics of Nonviolent Action* (1973)

79 Vorkuta 1953

In the coalmining camps at Vorkuta, there were a quarter of a million political prisoners living in poor conditions. The prisoners had for some time been speaking of the possibility of strike action against these. On Stalin's death in 1953, the prisoners were warned not to expect an amnesty which might endanger state security.

By the end of May, strike committees were secretly set up in several of the camps. They comprised for the most part Leninists, anarchists, and an interesting group called the *Monashki*, a Christian pacifist group which had arisen spontaneously since the revolution, and has been compared to the early Quakers. While this was happening, Beria, the infamous head of the secret police, fell, and this encouraged some of those uncertain whether to join. It was agreed that there should be a strike to demand abolition of the prison camps, and a change of status among the prisoners to freely contracted colonists.

The movement was by now an open secret. The authorities arrested the ringleaders and transported them to Moscow. This only had the effect of reinforcing the resolve of those who remained. A new committee was formed.

On July 21 the strike began, many of the prisoners refusing to go to work, and asking to present their demands personally to the general in command. By July 23, 30,000 were on strike. The general saw the leaders and made a response "containing vague promises and specific threats".

For a week nothing happened. The main threat to the strikers lay in the possible shortage of food supplies. The strikers intensified their activities. By now they had the sympathy of many of the soldiers on guard-duty who helped them to deliver strike leaflets. Twenty major coal pits had to close.

The authorities retaliated by replacing the Russian-speaking troops with soldiers from the Far East who did not speak Russian, and were less liable to have their sympathies attracted. The strike continued. In early August, the State Prosecutor arrived from Moscow with a posse of high-ranking officers and offered a number of minor concessions (two letters home a month instead of one; one visitor a year; removal of identification number from clothes; removal of iron bars from windows). The strike committee rejected these as cosmetic. The Prosecutor stepped up the concessions: better food; higher pay; shorter shifts. The strikers for the most part held firm. The leaders went for an interview with the commanding officer, never to return: they were deported or executed. Still the strikers held firm. They continued till late October, when shortage of food and fuel forced them to give way. But their stand had its effect, and far greater material improvements followed, and affected other camps as well as their own.

Sources: J. Scholmer, *Vorkuta*;
M. Sibley, *The Quiet Battle*;
G. Sharp, *The Politics of Nonviolent Action*

80 Nonviolence in East Germany

On 17 June 1953, the workers in East Germany began a strike against the Soviet-supported totalitarian regime of Walther Ulbricht. Organization was good; within a week there were strikes in 350 townships involving about half the working population. Their models were Georges Sorel and Mahatma Gandhi; they tried to apply Gandhi's *satyagraha* within a revolutionary activism; captured weapons were locked in a storeroom and not used. They stood in principle for the avoidance of bloodshed, and in practice hoped to avert Soviet intervention. In actual fact, Polish tanks were at first sent in, but the Polish officers refused to fire on unarmed nonviolent demonstrators. Then the Russian army moved in. Even then the Russian troops refused to fire, and some Russian officers sided with the strikers; other troops seemed to have fired when commanded, but to have deliberately fired wide. It was largely where the workers turned to violence against the Russians that the counter-violence prevailed.

The account is seemingly one of failure. Yet (a) the East Germans were not trained and disciplined in nonviolence, and it is hard to know how much further the revolt might have got had it been consistently nonviolent; (b) the uprising did in fact win reforms not merely in East Germany but in other Eastern European countries; (c) the experience of Hungary in 1956 shows the ruthlessness with which armed revolt was suppressed.

Source: *Non-Violent Action: A Christian Appraisal*

81 Desegregating a Cinema

The Fellowship of Reconciliation in the US felt that their witness for international reconciliation was invalid unless they could achieve reconciliation in their own community. In one town in the cinemas, by tradition, Blacks sat downstairs, Whites upstairs. They set themselves to break this practice. A group, including Blacks and Whites, paid for their tickets and all moved upstairs. The usherette stared at them in horror, and refused to admit them, sending for the manager. He sent for the police. Meantime a large queue was building up behind them. The police arrested them. But they were breaking custom, not law. They were charged therefore with blocking a legitimate passageway. They had no difficulty in showing that it was the manager who created the roadblock. They were released and went straight back to the same cinema, and again bought tickets, and again went upstairs. The manager was recalled, shrugged his shoulders and admitted them. Every day that week they paid to see the same film. Next week they sent the Blacks without the Whites. There was no trouble. By this method they desegregated every cinema in the town.

Source: Personal knowledge.

82 The Montgomery Bus Boycott and After

On 1 December 1955 in Montgomery, Alabama, USA, Mrs Rosa Parks, a black seamstress, was seated in a bus in a seat among those designated for coloured people, tired after her day's work. The bus filled up, and Mrs Parks was told to give up her seat to a white passenger. She refused and was arrested. In response to this arrest the local black community organized itself into the simplest of all nonviolent actions. They boycotted the buses until these should be desegregated.

The Dexter Avenue Baptist pastor was Martin Luther King, a third-generation preacher, who had been influenced by the social gospel of Walter Rauschenbusch, the political analysis of Reinhold Niebuhr, and the nonviolence of Mahatma Gandhi. King was almost forced into a position of leadership. He preached the love-ethic of Jesus. He refused retaliation for white violence (which included bombing). He identified six principles of Christian nonviolence. First, it is the way of the strong, not the weak; it is not stagnant passivity or do-nothing; it is an active, nonviolent resistance to evil. Second, its goal is reconciliation and redemption, and the creation of the beloved community. Third, it is directed against the forces of evil, not against people; it does not seek victory of one group over another, but of light over darkness. Fourth, it involves the acceptance of suffering without retaliation: "We will match your capacity to inflict suffering with our capacity to endure suffering." Fifth, the root of the action is *agape*, Christian love. Sixth, if there is faith in God, nonviolent love will in the end win: the universe is on the side of justice.

So the Blacks of Montgomery walked or, if they were lucky, bicycled. For days, weeks, months, they walked. One woman said proudly: "It used to be my soul was tired and my feets rested; now my feets is tired, but my soul is rested." Another was asked by the White family for whom she cooked whether she

137

supported the terrible things the Negroes were doing. "Oh, no, ma'am," she answered. "I am just going to stay away from the buses as long as that trouble is going on." After 382 days the US Supreme Court ruled the racial segregation on Alabama's buses unconstitutional. Martin Luther King and Glenn Smiley, a White worker for the Fellowship of Reconciliation, who had backed him and stood by him, rode the bus seated side by side.

The victory of Montgomery was a victory of the whole Negro people. Martin Luther King went on to other campaigns. The pledge taken by his followers is important.

1. *Meditate* daily on the teachings and life of Jesus.

2. *Remember* always that the non-violent movement in Birmingham seeks justice and reconciliation, not victory.

3. *Walk and talk* in the manner of love, for God is love.

4. *Pray* daily to be used by God in order that all men might be free.

5. *Sacrifice* personal wishes in order that all men might be free.

6. *Observe* with both friend and foe the ordinary rules of courtesy.

7. *Seek* to perform regular service for others and for the world.

8. *Refrain* from the violence of fist, tongue, or heart.

9. *Strive* to be in good spiritual and bodily health.

10. *Follow* the directions of the movement and of the captain of the demonstration.

He moved into the segregated state of Georgia. At Albany he failed. But in Birmingham, Alabama, he faced the tough Commissioner of Public Safety, "Bull" Connor.

Bull Connor secured an injunction against King and his fellows. They broke the injunction. Four hundred went to jail. King wrote his famous "Letter from Birmingham Jail" justifying the breaking of unjust laws. True peace is not the absence of tension but the presence of justice. Children began to join in marches, 6,000 of them. A thousand young demonstrators were set upon by Connor and his police with fire hoses, batons and dogs. Some Blacks retaliated, but the core of the movement was nonviolent. Two thousand were arrested, but more and more marched. A settlement was reached: the desegregation of facilities in the stores, and of reserved jobs, the release of prisoners, and provision for regular communication between the racial groups. The settlement caused a backlash. A Black Sunday School was bombed, and four little girls killed. Black extremists argued for counter-violence, but one of the fathers cried, "I'm not for that. What good would Denise have done with a machine gun in her hand?"

King received the Nobel Peace Prize. He now began to protest against the Vietnam war, and to engage in a Poor People's Campaign, not just for Blacks but for Puerto Ricans, Mexican Indians, Appalachian Whites. He was campaigning for garbage-collectors when he was shot.

His dream lives on:

I have a dream that my four little children one day will live in a nation where they will not be judged by the colour of their skin, but by the content of their character...

When we allow freedom to ring from every town and every hamlet, from every state and from every city, we will be able to speed up that day when all of God's children, black men and white men, Jews and Gentiles, Protestants and Catholics, will be able to join hands and say in the words of the old Negro spiritual 'Free at last! Free at last! Great God Almighty, we are free at last.'

Sources:
M. L. King *Stride Towards Freedom*; *Why We Can't Wait*;
Coretta Scott King, *My Life with Martin Luther King Jr.*;
K. Slack *Martin Luther King*;
personal knowledge.

83 Why didn't they hit back?

Eddie Dickerson was a young lad in the small town of Cambridge, Maryland, who left school at sixteen, drifted round for six years, tough, restless, often getting into fights.

The Congress of Racial Equality (CORE), a nonviolent organization which had done much firmly and gently to desegregate lunch counters, sent a group of ten Negroes and twenty Whites to nearby Easton, warning the authorities. They tested the restaurants with mixed groups. Eight seated and served them. Six refused. These they picketed. Now gangs began to attack them. Eddie Dickerson and his brother Joe came over to join in. Eddie was armed with kicking boots and brass knuckle-dusters.

As they drove back they were laughing about what they'd done. But Eddie was obsessed by the vision of the people he'd hit: "Why the hell didn't they get mad and hit back?"

He stopped the car and walked back to Easton. He knocked on the door of the church they were staying in. The door opened. He said, "I reckon you don't know me." Bill Hansen, who was at the door, said "Yeah, you're the one who beat me up a couple of hours ago." They expected to be mobbed by a gang, but Eddie walked in alone. It was he who said, "I want to know what's going on. I hit you and you didn't hit me. I came back here by myself. You could mob me now and really pound into me, but you don't. Why not?" Bill said, "Well, you're here. That's the reason. We want to reach people and make them understand." They talked far into the night.

A week later the CORE group went to Cambridge, picketed some restaurants, and were arrested. Eddie dressed neatly and went to the courthouse. The whole case was rigged and unjust. He was furious, and reached out to shake hands with one of the CORE people who happened to be coloured. An officer grabbed him saying, "Let go! You're nuts, shaking hands with a nigger." He answered, scarcely knowing what he was saying, "So what? He's my friend."

When Eddie reached home his father and his brothers threw him out. His old friends beat him up. There was a move to have him committed to a mental asylum. It was the CORE people who looked after him and found him work. He said later that they alone treated him with dignity, no matter what he did. Through them he came to believe that there was more to life than drifting around in gang-fights; he began to read, to train, and to practise nonviolence.

Source: A. Paul Hare and H. H. Blumberg
Nonviolent Direct Action

84 The Strike-in-reverse

Danilo Dolci, an architect, came from Trieste to Sicily to
see the ancient Greek temples. He found an area of bitter
poverty—waste of land through erosion, waste of water, waste
of humanity through illness, unemployment, poor housing, lack
of education, destitution and crime. In 1953 over a quarter of the
people of Sicily were destitute. Out of 814 people in one area were
7 cases of meningitis, 42 of typhus, 105 of tuberculosis. The week
Dolci arrived, a child died of starvation.

Dolci settled among them, married a village woman, and
turned their home into the centre of the fight against poverty,
ignorance and prejudice. His vision was of the *Borgo di Dio*, the
Village of God.

Among the things Danilo has done, four stand out.

First, he has defied the Mafia, the criminals who dominate
Sicily. He has denounced them and exposed their crimes. But
he will not protect himself against by violence and arms. His
protection is his commitment to God—and with that the fact
that the people love him.

Secondly, he has devised an original weapon of nonviolence to
fight unemployment. He calls it the strike in reverse. A strike is
the withdrawal of labour. In the strike in reverse you work when
others try to stop you. So the unemployed people have built roads
and dams and schools, although the government has tried to stop
them. And they have won.

Thirdly, like Gandhi, he fasts for righteousness. "How can
I eat," he said, "when I see so many little eyes watching me,
full of envy and hunger?" So he fasted and others joined him,
and they moved the conscience of those in power.

Fourthly, he believes in the good sense of the people, in open
discussion. The result is that his work does not depend on himself
alone. It is a movement of the people, a grassroots movement.

Source: J. Ferguson *Danilo Dolci*;
Danilo Dolci's own writings.

85 The Scene in South Africa

Events in South Africa form an important though tragically inconclusive area of study. The scene is complex, with the White ruling minority divided between the English-speakers and Afrikaans-speakers, both wedded to White supremacy, but the one more pragmatic and the other more dogmatic; a large group technically known as Coloureds, descendants of mixed unions; a sizeable body of Indians; and the African majority, politically dispossessed and economically underprivileged.

Gandhi had carried out his first experiments with peace in South Africa, and his example was in the background of the founding of the African National Congress in 1912. One of the chief symbols of oppression was the police pass, which Black Africans had to carry at all times. The ANC made continual political representations without effect. There were occasional demonstrations against this or other evils, but they were spasmodic, disorganized and ineffectual.

With the election in 1948 of a government committed to apartheid, the ANC turned aside from talk and committed itself to a programme of strike action and civil disobedience. The espousal of nonviolence was governed partly by the immediate example of the Indians, though without any special commitment to the ethical philosophy of *satyagraha*, partly by expediency, and partly by a sense that this was the logical next stage. But there was strong Christian leadership in the campaign itself, and many of the demonstrating groups demonstrated through massed prayer; Albert Luthuli, who later became President of ANC, held to nonviolence out of Christian conviction.

A systematic campaign was started on 26 June 1952, being preceded by mass rallies in some of the main centres of population. The main target was the counters and facilities marked "For Europeans Only". The campaign was highly disciplined, courteous and by and large firm. It lasted for exactly a year, at the end of which it had clearly failed at least for the time being. There were three reasons for the failure. First, though the rallies had attracted tens of thousands of people, the number of volunteers prepared to accept the discipline of nonviolent action leading to prison was disappointingly small. By October it had reached only 2354, and two months later it had declined to a few hundred, and at Johannesberg no volunteers

143

could be found to take up the work of those under arrest. Nonviolent methods are unlikely to get far unless they are used on a larger scale by greater numbers of committed and dedicated people. Secondly, the President of ANC, Dr Moroka, broke discipline and compromised with the government. Thirdly, 18 October saw a series of violent riots bloodily suppressed. These riots were nothing to do with the campaign, and there is some reason to think that they were instigated by government *agents provocateurs*. These gave the government the excuse for harshly repressive measures.

In 1958 the Pan-African Congress was established as a more activist rival to ANC, and in 1960 it launched a new campaign. The commitment was still nonviolent; large numbers of Africans deliberately sought arrest for breaking the pass-laws. At Sharpeville on 21 March a crowd of 7,000 massed for a nonviolent demonstration. Through tear-gas attacks and the threat of armoured cars they remained disciplined and nonviolent. Then, after some hours, one or two broke discipline and began to throw stones. The police promptly fired 476 bullets on the crowd, killing sixty-seven people. On 30 March, 30,000 Africans marched in nonviolent protest through the streets of Capetown. Promises were made by the authorities; the marchers dispersed peaceably: the promises were broken; and a campaign of police terrorism followed. This too was met with nonviolence, and Norman Phillips, an American missionary who was present, who compared the actions of the police with those of the Gestapo in the Warsaw ghettos, said that only nonviolence prevented massacre.

The evidence from South Africa is inconclusive. Three things are however clear. First, the government does not know how to deal with nonviolent action. This was clear at Capetown. It is when nonviolence has turned to violence that it has been most ruthlessly suppressed. Hence the use of *agents provocateurs*. Second, nonviolence will not succeed unless there are large numbers of people willing to accept its discipline. Third, though the numbers are still small, some White South Africans are refusing the draft because they would be liable to be used in an unjust military action against the Blacks.

Source: *Violence in Southern Africa* (1970); L. Kuper, *Passive Resistance in South Africa*; A. Luthuli, *Let My People Go*

86 Cesar Chavez and the California Farmworkers

The San Joaquin valley stretches with its broad flat floor 600 miles from the Sierra Nevada westwards. In the dry period it seems a huge desert, but the winter waters flood and fertilize the extensive vineyards. Here was an area of bitter exploitation of the bowed backs of the workers. But in 1939, came Liberado and Juana Chavez with their son Cesar.

In 1953 Cesar was twenty-five. Fred Ross asked his help in organizing a Community Service Chapter. At first he could not believe that a white man would care about Mexicans. He threw aside his mistrust, worked hard for the CSO, and in ten years became its national Director. He learned from Fred Ross; Fred Ross had learned from Saul Alinsky, one of the great practical prophets of nonviolent resistance.

The farmworkers had no unions to protect them. Agriculture is the biggest big business in California. Cesar gave up a safe job to move to Delano, and give himself for the protection of the workers. He planned wisely, developing a network of housegroups across the years till he had a firm basis for united action. Even so the challenge came before he believed they were ready to face it. In 1965 the challenge could not be resisted. The workers came out on strike.

Chavez is a dedicated Christian. He knew that the strikers would be faced with intolerable hardship unless they were sustained by a movement of the Spirit. Prayer and fasting were central to *La Causa*. The journeying of the people became a pilgrimage, led by the banner of the Virgin. Spirituality and political action went hand in hand.

Because he is a dedicated Christian, and a practical man, he insisted on nonviolence: "I am convinced that the truest act of courage, the strongest act of manliness is to sacrifice ourselves for others in a totally nonviolent struggle for justice. To be a man is to suffer for others. God help us to be men."

When the strikers were tempted to violence, Chavez called off all action for twenty-one days while he fasted. He took all the violence on to himself.

They faced scabs and mobsters, violence, hunger, all the prejudice of rich against poor, owners against workers, whites against those of other races. But the organization, still in its youth, held firm.

Two techniques were used. One was the secondary boycott. The workers left their homes to go to every large city in the US and man the entrances to the supermarkets to persuade the people not to buy Californian table grapes till conditions of work improved. After five years of strike action and a shorter period of boycott, the Giumarra contract was signed in 1970.

Then they used the orthodox political machinery to help to secure the election of Jerry Brown as Governor in 1974. Governor Brown secured for them the right to organize in unions.

Source: *Reconciliation Quarterly*, March 1981.

87 The Vietnamese Buddhists

The 1930s saw in Vietnam a rising tide of violence against the French, and a reformation of Buddhism in Vietnam with a strong commitment to peace and social welfare. Since then, the country has been the scene of a power struggle between left and right with considerable involvement from powers outside. The Buddhists were not prepared to see Vietnam sacrificed to the international interests of Communists or Anti-Communists. They stood against the suppression of opposition by the left and the exploitation of the poor by the right, and the violence of both sides.

The Vietnamese Buddhists chose a quite different way from the left-wing monks of China and Burma and consistently sought to oppose both the tyranny of the Thieu regime and the violence of the communists by nonviolent means. The culmination came when a monk, Thich Quang-Duc, burnt himself to death on 11 June 1963 and others followed suit. Thich Nhat Hanh, in his book *Vietnam: The Lotus in the Sea of Fire*, expounded the meaning of the act. It is an extension of the act of the ordinand who burns a small spot on his body. It is a proof of the seriousness of his dedication and his measure. He is enduring the greatest sufferings to protect his people. Thich Quang-Duc's act was not suicide in the normal sense, arising from a sense of defeat and loss of hope. It was an act of construction, not of destruction. It was comparable with an action told of the Buddha in a former existence, who gave himself to a hungry lioness to save her from eating her own cubs. It was an act of compassion.

Thich Nhat Hanh himself is a poet who has expressed his nonviolent philosophy in powerful verse:

Men cannot be our enemies—even men called "Vietcong!"
If we kill men, what brothers will we have left?
With whom shall we live then?

Condemnation

Even as they
strike you down
with a mountain of hate and violence...
remember brother,
remember
man is not our enemy.

Recommendation

Thich Nhat Hanh wrote to Martin Luther King: "I believe with all my heart that the monks who burned themselves did not aim at the death of the oppressors but only at a change in their policy. Their enemies are not man. They are intolerance, fanaticism, dictatorship, cupidity, hatred and discrimination which lie within the heart of man...These are the real enemies of man—not man himself. In our unfortunate fatherland we are trying to plead desperately; do not kill man, even in man's name. Please kill the real enemies of man which are present everywhere, in our very hearts and minds."

Source: Thich Nhat Hanh, *The Lotus in the Sea of Fire*; · personal knowledge

148

88 The Czechs face Russian Invasion

In August 1968, half a million Russian troops invaded Czechoslovakia. Military resistance would in any event have been hopeless. The Czechs did not even attempt it; the troops remained in barracks. The Russians abducted Alexander Dubcek and other Czech leaders. The Russians expected within four days to impose a puppet government on a docile people. It took eight months.

The nonviolent resistance which followed the invasion was unplanned and improvised. President Svoboda refused to sign a document presented to him. Employees of the news agency refused to put out a statement declaring that the Russians had been invited in by the Czechs. Ministers of government and officials of the Communist Party declared that the invasion was without their knowledge or consent. The National Assembly demanded "the release from detention of our constitutional representatives" and "the immediate withdrawal of the armies ". The clandestine radio network called for one-hour general strikes, and action by railworkers to slow up Russian movements. They constantly urged firmness and nonviolence; violence was futile and dangerous. Many of the police supported the nonviolent resistance.

The Soviet authorities tried to get Svoboda to negotiate. He refused to do so except in company with the abducted leaders. This had to be granted by the Russians, and a compromise left most of the leaders and withdrew some of the extreme Russian demands, though some of the reforms were abandoned, and Russian troops were left. It was touch and go whether the people would accept the compromise. For a full week they refused; then they agreed. The reformists and important parts of the reforms to which the Russians objected remained.

They remained till April 1969, when the nonviolent discipline at length gave way—it is thought through the activity of *agents provocateurs*—and this offered the Russians an excuse for a heavier clampdown.

So nonviolent resistance in the end failed in the immediate situation. But it is right to keep things in proportion. Gene Sharp wrote well, "Had unprepared military struggle against such odds held off the Russians for eight months it would have been hailed by the West as victory even in defeat, with courage and historical significance comparable to Thermopylae." Russian plans expected Czech military resistance and calculated to crush it in four days. Improvised nonviolent action held them off for eight months, and left no legacy of death and a smaller legacy of bitterness.

Sources: Gene Sharp, *The Politics of Nonviolent Action*;
Bulletin of Peace Proposals, 9.4 (1978);
Peace News, 3.4 1981

89 Hungary

There has been a curious parallel between Hungary in the nineteenth and twentieth centuries. In the nineteenth, Ferenc Deak achieved by nonviolence what Louis Kossuth had failed to achieve by violence. Both remain national heroes. In 1956 the Hungarians rose violently against Russian dominated oppression, and were crushed by Russian tanks.

Over the next three decades the Hungarians learned to use different techniques. There has been no individual heroic leader, but there have been subtle changes. Hungary remains a one-party state. But it is not necessary to belong to the party to attain high responsibility, and even within the party, if you ask whether all party members are Marxist-Leninist you will be greeted with roars of laughter. The churches say that they have passed from confrontation through coexistence to cooperation, and that they are in fruitful dialogue with the Marxist leaders; the State publishing house is actually publishing some Christian literature. The year 1985 saw free elections for the first time, with candidates chosen openly in village meetings and the like, followed by a process of secret ballot. The economy has been liberalized, and there is an interesting combination of state control and free enterprise. There is no obviously oppressive police presence, and no bugging of restaurant tables (as in some countries). People speak their minds freely.

The Hungarians stand for a nuclear-free zone in central Europe, and would like to see themselves as a moderating voice within the Warsaw Treaty Organization.

They have considerable sympathy for the Solidarity movement in Poland, but say "we plead with them not to try to do in three years what has taken us thirty."

Nonviolence may work slowly, but it works. This, in its way, is a real revolution.

Source: Personal knowledge

90 UN Peace Keeping

The UN peace-keeping operations form a study of particular interest. The forces involved comprise a mixture of professional and volunteer soldiers supplied by UN member states. They do not, of course, enter a country except by invitation of the government, but it is fundamental that they are independent and do not in any sense represent the government inviting them. They are there to observe, mediate and keep the peace; they do not take sides in the dispute; and though they are soldiers and, as such, armed, they do not use their weapons except in self-defence, and some critics regard even that exception as dangerous. They form to all intents and purposes a disciplined nonviolent force of intervention and conciliation. Observers on their own can do a great deal; fifty UN observers on the Kashmir frontier kept the peace between India and Pakistan. In the Middle East a frontier force of 6,000 kept the peace for ten years; the great success of peace keeping in Cyprus was achieved by about 4,000 men. They made economic relief possible; they enabled the normal and essential work of farming to go on in both the Greek and Turkish areas. When a Greek army was advancing on the Turkish village of Melousha, the UN peace keepers stood in their path and said "Over our dead bodies"; the Greeks fell back. When there were communal murders round Paphos, the UN force quickly made the area safe for movement and drew the disputants together. The force was, in Brigadier Harbottle's word, "enmeshed" in the ordinary communal life around it. "Its weapons are negotiation, mediation, quiet diplomacy, tact and patient reasoning, and, above all, an understanding of the human relationships involved and of the structural causes of the conflict." The UN experience is important, because it demonstrates the possibility of a use of nonviolence, not only in the meeting of aggression or the remedying of social injustice, but in mediation in a conflict by a third party.

Sources: M. Harbottle, *The Blue Berets*;
The Impartial Soldier;
UN publications; personal knowledge.

91 The Shanti Sena at Ahmeda Bay

The Shanti Sena is a group dedicated in the spirit of Gandhi to the use of nonviolent methods either to transform a situation of violence or to produce revolutionary, that is fundamental, change. They work for a new society based on a sense of the value of each individual, of equality in the control of community life, and of justice.

In September 1969, communal riots in Ahmenabad left 2,000 dead and vast stretches of the city ravaged by fire. There were historical reasons for the conflict, accentuated by almost accidental events and a vast growth of rumour—about the killing of temple cows, the molestation of women, the slashing of a woman's breasts, the desecration of temple images, the poisoning of milk—all false. There were three waves of violence.

There were only a few Shanti Sainiks living in Ahmedabad. They did what they could but were unable to stem the tide of violence. But now Shanti Sainiks poured into the city and set to work. The problems were immense. Apart from the destruction and destitution there was exploitation of the poor by the landlords. The majority community showed no penitence. The young of both communities had grown up in hostility. Political leaders had their eyes on the elections. Everyone was blaming everyone else.

Under the guidance of the Shanti Sena student volunteers set themselves to clear the debris, make contact with the people and restore goodwill. There were house-to-house visitations. Hindus were persuaded to visit the camps of Muslim refugees and invite them to their homes. Shanti Sena supervised the rebuilding of houses, an easy area for dishonesty, and the distribution of blankets. In the face of jealousy from other relief organizations, and a certain amount of practical hostility, by organizing a committee of women workers from all communities, they were able to rehabilitate those widowed through the riots. They helped in the rehabilitation of street traders.

Alongside this, less immediately but ultimately more importantly, they had to dispel the hatred. They published a weekly called *Insan* (*Human Being*) which became something of a bestseller. They organized a kind of systematic graffiti on wallboards throughout the city under the title *Ektane Panthe* (*The Road to Unity*). Nonviolent leaders, including the Hindu Jayaprakash Narayan and the Muslim Abdul Ghaffar Khan, visited the city. They celebrated the latter's birthday as the Day for Human Fellowship. They persuaded people of all communities to join in the Muslim Id festival. They enrolled a thousand volunteers to give time to peace making. On 30 January they organized six large processions, including thousands of Muslim women; the marchers cried "We may be Hindus, we may be Muslims, but above all we are human beings." The anniversary of Gandhi's death was turned into a Day of Peace.

Source: Narayan Desai in
A. P. Hare and H. H. Blumberg
Liberation Without Violence

92 Culebra

Culebra is a little island, part of Puerto Rican territory, perhaps the original of Stevenson's Treasure Island. Since the 1930s it had been "a keystone in the Atlantic Fleet weapons range" for the US, a bombing and gunnery practice ground. Already, in 1935, the first Culebran life was lost through live ammunition lying around; loss of limbs or blindness was not uncommon. In 1941 there was demolition of houses and a Methodist chapel at forty-eight hours notice. Calebran protests were by and large ignored or trivialized: "Thank you for expressing your feelings on this subject to the President." In 1959 the shelling averaged nine and a half hours every weekday and three and a half hours on Sunday; in 1970 it went beyond even that.

The Puerto Rican Independence Party, committed to non-violent action, began to act nonviolently. They staged a swim-in on Flamingo Beach, defying the guns, sleeping on the sand. On 10 June 1970, twenty Culebrans stood on the target area where shelling was about to begin. Navy personnel pleaded with the group to withdraw. They stood firm: it was the ship which withdrew.

The Mayor was afraid that the failure to achieve radical change might lead to violence. The Navy tried to win the Culebrans by offering well-paid jobs for guarding the beach, but this only generated more antagonism. In December the Navy killed thousands of fish, destroyed fifty feet of coral reef and damaged two hundred feet more in the course of underwater demolition. The next such operation was picketed by three Culebran boats. The commander gave the order to detonate. Two of the boats retreated, one, brought by three women, stayed, and had to be towed away.

Meantime, with the support of a Quaker contingent, there were plans to rebuild the chapel destroyed thirty years before. These were announced on 4 January 1971 two weeks before a major naval exercise involving 70 ships, 180 planes and 60,000 troops. Suddenly the Navy came up with what they first termed

155

a "peace treaty" (they later deleted the words). The Navy would phase out all targets except the northwest peninsula and avoid week-end operations; the Culebrans would not intervene in the north-west. If the Culebrans did not agree, the Navy would deny the offer had been made. A hasty public meeting was called, and in the final vote, after inadequate discussion, about 50 were for and 6 against. The Culebrans were unhappy. False promises were made, and there was an attempt to bulldoze the thing through. The protesters said that what was offered was bombing by consent. The construction of a fence, designed to make the matter a *fait accompli*, was taken as an affront.

The rebuilding of the chapel in the target area came next, with a dedicatory service. Six members stayed on the site and were arrested. Four more demonstrators entered the target area, and firing was halted while they were pursued. One night the chapel was bulldozed. The Culebrans rebuilt it. Religious services were held on the beach. One confrontation led to violence on both sides; mercifully there was only one minor casualty. The Marines destroyed the chapel yet again.

At the trial the defendants were sentenced to three months' imprisonment but were able to make a notable witness against war, militarism and violence. The result was an intensification of nonviolent action. By 31 March the Navy were beginning to give way. In April it was announced that all naval activities would be moved from Culebra by mid-1975 and transferred to uninhabited islands. All gunfire training ceased there on 30 June 1975.

Fifty-two Culebrans decided to rebuild the chapel as a symbol of the people's successful resistance under God. They were arrested, but the building was completed. This time it was left to stand.

Source: Charles Walker in
A. P. Hare and H. H. Blumberg
Liberation Without Violence

93 The Perus Strike

In the suburbs of Sao Paolo in Brazil, there is a Perus cement factory. Nine hundred workmen were suffering from the withholding of pay for several months in arrears, as well as intolerable conditions of work. They decided that the only way of resolving this situation was a policy of non-cooperation and withdrawal of labour. They found that they had all those in power united against them: employers, politicians, police, military, press, the Church. They were described as Communists, subversives, traitors; they were denounced, falsely accused, imprisoned, tortured, killed. But through imprisonment, persecution and hardship they remained firm. It took seven years of strike action, and twelve lawsuits.

Their action was governed by three cardinal principles.

First, it was nonviolent. At first this was the result of necessity. Their oppressors held all the weapons. If they had turned to violence they would have been crushed. But then as good Catholics they turned to the New Testament and began to cry, "But it's all here!" So a necessity became a commitment. They called for seminars on nonviolence, training in nonviolence.

Second, they insisted on maintaining dialogue with their oppressors, indeed with anyone they could reach: "the Boss and all the groups supporting the status quo; the uncommitted, the press, the Church, the lawyers, the middle classes, the police, the prison authorities." They refused to be dragged into a "we- they" mentality:

> He drew a circle which shut me out -
> Heretic, rebel, a thing to flout.
> But Love and I had the wit to win.
> We drew a circle which took him in.

They said constantly to their oppressors: "You may kill us, but the justice we defend will continue to advance till injustice is vanquished."

Third, they sought maximum publicity for their case and their actions. At first there was difficulty over this. But they went to the episcopal conference, and won a bishop to their side, then thirty-five bishops, and access to the Catholic press. Eventually the largest paper in Sao Paolo *O Estado de Sao Paolo* agreed to state their position.

The turning point came when blackleg gangsters set out to drive the cement lorries. The strikers pleaded with them unavailingly, then lay down in the path of the lorries. The police stood by, idle or jeering. The blacklegs started their engines and let in the clutches. The strikers lay unmoving. And now, faced with the spectacle of men who would die for justice but not kill or hate, the police intervened. They leaped on the lorries and checked the drivers.

And at the twelfth lawsuit, in 1974 the boss was compelled to pay the workers 15 million cruseiros.

Source: *Reconciliation Quarterly*, June 1977;
oral information.

94 Toctezinin 1974

A law passed in Ecuador provides that the land cultivated by peasants by their own means and for their own needs, becomes the property of those peasants. The only trouble was that the government did not publish the rules for application. At Toctezinin, the chief landowner ignored the law, with the backing of the political authorities. When the peasants protested, many were arrested, false evidence was prefered against them, and one, Lazaro Condo, was assassinated.

The peasants determined to remain firmly nonviolent and refused to be provoked into counter-violence. More, they organized seminars and training-schools so as to discipline themselves to the practice of nonviolence. They met threats with unflinching calm, lies with a total and truthful openness.

The peasants steadfastly clung to their land. The attempts to oust them were met by letters, delegations and conversations. They rejected a narrow polarization. The issue moved outside the locality, to the nation, outside the nation to the whole of Latin America.

In this they received considerable support from Monsignor Preano and the pastoral team he had developed. Monsignor Preano is a firm believer in social awareness and liberation guided by New Testament values. He kept the issues before the whole country by means of the Church radio and would not permit the voice of the peasants to be silenced. The peasants were growing in solidarity. They began to harvest communally. There were mass arrests. The pastoral team, and even the Vicar-General of the diocese, was arrested with the peasants. For once the Church was where the Church should be, suffering with the poor and oppressed. at this stage, Monsignor Preano succeeded in getting an audience with the Minister of Agriculture. The government intervened. The land legislation was brought into effective action. The peasants received their due.

Source: *Reconciliation Quarterly*, June 1977.

95 Alagamar

Alagamar is a region of north-east Brazil. It was suddenly discovered that sugar cane could provide alcohol to be added to gasoline. The value of the land on which sugar cane could be grown escalated. A new proprietor, with an eye to the main chance, tried to expropriate the peasants.

This was an area of strongly developed Christian base communities, combining Christian faith, social action, a concern for justice and liberation from oppression, and nonviolence. The peasants consulted a lawyer, who advised them that the land they tilled was theirs, and that measures to expel them were illegal.

The peasants had built a large chapel and community centre of mudbrick. They gathered here and decided to resist. The proprietor sent his security guards and destroyed the chapel. Dom Jóse Maria, Archbishop of Joao Pessoa, heard of this and came the very next Sunday to celebrate the Eucharist among the ruins with a congregation of several hundreds.

The peasants tried to negotiate with the proprietor, but he evaded them. They invoked the law. In consequence they were persecuted and calumniated; some were arrested and imprisoned. The rest rallied in solidarity with them, marched to the town and the judge's house and demanded all to be arrested. In the end they were all set free.

They began to plant collective fields of mandioca. The proprietor sent an armed force to pull up the plants. The men affected came together, reaffirmed their principles ("First, never kill; second, never hurt; third, remain always united"), and watched in silent vigil while their persecutors uprooted 3,000 plants. Next day they replanted them, except for some which the Archbishop took to offer on the altar.

So others, who had been hostile to or aloof from the peasants, began to change. Who was subversive? The peasants, who stood by the law, were never provoked to hatred or violence, and stood for justice and fair shares for all, or the wealthy individuals and firms, who flouted the law, used private violence, and served their own ends?

Pressure increased. Public opinion was strong and vocal. The President of the Republic came to the area, and handed over a quarter of the land to the peasants for their exclusive use.

Sources: *Reconciliation Quarterly*, June 1980;
Solidarity, March 1984.

96 The Weapon of the Poor

Bolivia is one of the poorest of the Latin American countries. In the 1970s, it was ruled by a dictatorship unsympathetic to those at the bottom of the social pyramid.

In 1977 the mining centre of Catavi-Siglo II was the scene of grave oppression. The mineworkers were overworked and underpaid. When they protested, the forces of state power were massed against them. Protesting workers were dismissed, trades unions were banned, and the army sent in to maintain "order".

Four women trekked 500 kilometres to the capital city of La Paz. Their seventeen children were with them. They went to the house of the Catholic archbishop, and there they began a hunger strike. Sympathy grew for their cause, and before long more than a thousand people, rich and poor, men, women and children, aristocrats and business people and workers, had joined with them, and very many others came to support their demands.

Their demands were straightforward:

(a) General and unconditional amnesty.
(b) Restoration of dismissed workers. Permission for trade.
(c) Permission for trade unions to resume normal activity.
(d) Withdrawal of the army.

The hunger strike lasted twenty-one days. By that time, the support was so massive and formidable that the government had to give way, and all the workers' demands were conceded. It was not merely a triumph for social justice in a particular situation. It was a challenge to the absolute power of the dictatorship.

Today in Bolivia they speak of the periods "before the hunger strike" and "after the hunger strike".

Source: Adolfo Peres Esquivel,
Nonviolence: The Weapon of the Poor

97 Larzac—A Victory for Nonviolence

The Larzac, in France, is a limestone plateau, famed because Roquefort cheese is made nearby. Here in 1901 a military camp was established by agreement. It covered 500 hectares; a further 2500 hectares were available for army use, but were to be grazed by the farmers in the normal way. In October 1970 news leaked out of a plan to extend the camp by 14,000 hectares, closing 58 farms and affecting 40 more, and seriously reducing the supply of milk for Roquefort cheese, as well as threatening pollution, and serious damage to rare fauna, flora and prehistoric sites.

In September 1971, after various attempts to manipulate the situation from outside, the peasants decided to act themselves. First, in protest against the actions and attitude of the mayor, they dumped a load of manure on his doorstep. They came into Millau, six thousand in number, to demonstrate against the extension. They won the support of all but one of the local councils. They enrolled other organizations throughout the country. The authorities kept wriggling, promising one thing and slipping in another, representing the farms as derelict and the peasants as aged.

On 7 November 1971, a pastoral letter from the Bishop of Rodez expressed disquiet at the proposed development of military activity. On 1 March 1972, the Catholic disciple of Gandhi, Lanza del Vasto, founder of the Community of the Ark (a few miles away) spoke to an audience of one thousand, advocating nonviolent action. A week later Abbé Jean Toulat proposed nonviolent civilian defence. Lanza began a fast; many of the peasants shared it; and one hundred and three of them took a joint pledge not to sell their land to the army. Easter saw a large influx of marchers for peace and country folk from regions round about coming to see for themselves the vitality of the plateau people.

A public inquiry was held at short notice 16–30 October 1972. The peasants, in a brilliantly conceived action, took sixty ewes

163

with "Save the Larzac" on their fleeces to Paris, and set them to graze on the Champs de Mars below the Eiffel Tower, attracting excellent publicity. The Commission's conclusions were predetermined. The peasants now organized a "tractorcade" as far as Orléans, where they were stopped; they reached Paris by other means, and addressed a large meeting. They now began acts of civil disobedience, returning the military papers issued to conscripts; others elsewhere joined them in sympathy. They built a *bergerie* for five hundred ewes in La Blaquière, although it was in the area scheduled for extension, and a permit was refused. They organized an Association for the Development of Agriculture on the Larzac. In August 1973 there was a major demonstration of the peasant workers on the plateau, involving 80,000 people.

The army began buying land, but the farms they bought were dispersed and useless for manoeuvres. The peasants countered by establishing a Land Trust. In August 1974 there was a new rally attended by 100,000. A crop was harvested for the Third World. The slogan was "Arms Kill. Wheat Gives Life." Banners proclaimed, "Solidarity—Workers—Peasants—Third World." Unfortunately an incident in which the peasants were not concerned occurred involving François Mitterrand. It was minor, and such incidents were rare, but it received undue prominence.

Important events involved taking over some neglected farms designated for the military and farming them productively. Another important episode involved water supply. The authorities had offered piped water in compensation for the takeover. They brought the water to the plateau, but refused to connect it to the farms. The peasants took the law into their own hands, dug trenches, and connected it for themselves. Then there was a bomb outrage against one of the peasant leaders; this led to nationwide demonstrations for the peasants, and a reaffirmation of their stand by the 103 (now 102 in number; the personnel had suffered some changes).

The year 1976 saw some direct confrontations. Twenty-two peasants and sympathizers entered the camp and destroyed some files. They were sentenced lightly, and the episode won them support. Unfortunately, in one demonstration a gas canister thrown by a gendarme blinded a bystander in one eye—the only serious casualty in the whole campaign. Another confrontation had to do with the taking over of the farm of the Cavaliès. The squatters were evicted, and the farm turned into an army fortress with barbed wire entanglements and armed guards. This happened with four other farms, despite peasant attempts to maintain dialogue with the soldiers. This was most amusing when the army tried manoeuvres. The peasants blocked their progress and entered into dialogue with the conscripts, a situation which the regular officers viewed with growing unease. The army sometimes engaged in acts of vandalism against the peasants.

The decrees for the Army takeover were brought into law in 1978-9. This was answered by a national day of action, fasts if fifty towns, a letter to the President, and a major march from the Larzac to Paris. The President refused to meet them; they saw members of the Defence Ministry. The peasants argued for discussion of the real issues, no forcing of farmers from land they farmed, and the suspension of expropriation pending talks. As a result of these talks, the official position became clearer, and clearly ill thought out. Modifications were accepted, but the basic plan for turning a large area of the plateau into a military range was unchanged. The visit of the expropriation judge saw a nonviolent demonstration violently suppressed. The indifference to local opinion began to change the views of those in power locally.

Nonetheless, the evictions took place on 1 December 1980. But in 1981 Mitterrand was elected President. He was sympathetic to the peasants. On 2 June the new government received a delegation of peasants. On 3 June the Council of Ministers cancelled the project.

It should be added that, in August 1981, an International Meeting for Peace took place on the plateau, with ten foreign delegations including Afghan refugees, Latin Americans, and Japanese. After this the peasants sent a call to the French people to join in the movement against nuclear weapons, and to protest against the French nuclear weapons systems.

Source: R. Rawlinson, *Larzac—A Victory for Nonviolence*

98 Winterthur

In January 1981, it was announced that an international arms exhibition was to be held at Winterthur in Switzerland the following summer. Constitutional protests were ignored. The City Council claimed to be bound by contract.

The objectors then began a campaign of education. Street theatre and information booths were set up to inform the public just what the arms trade meant. White crosses by the hundred were set up in the City Park. A large demonstration of 3,000 with a march was mainly peaceful, but some support was lost when some paint was thrown and display windows broken.

When the exhibition began the organizers resolved not to make that mistake. It must be totally nonviolent. A small group stood by to make contact with those passing. The rest, some 50 on the first day, lay interlocked to form a human carpet. Delegations drove up, and drove away again. A hostile public was won over by the refusal of provocation.

On the second day the police used water cannons to disperse the "carpet". Ironically, the floods of water deterred prospective visitors to the exhibition.

By the fourth day there were some arrests, but the human carpet was maintained. Discipline broke momentarily on the fifth when liquid manure was poured over them, but they soon regained their composure and good humour.

The total result was that visitors to the exhibition fell from and expected 10,000 to 3,000, and that many of the general public were challenged by the evils of the arms trade and by the positive power of sincere conviction acting nonviolently and willing to suffer.

Source: *Reconciliation Quarterly*, September 1983

99 Chile 1986

The key is *rélampago* (lightning) action. Demonstrators converge on an agreed point at an agreed time, with crowds around. Observers are stationed around. Friendly journalists are alerted. At the given time banners are raised *NO A LA TORTURA* and *NO A LA DICTADURA*. Handbills are distributed. Five minutes later the demonstrators disappear. Sometimes the police and military arrive too early: then the demonstrators experience the things against which they are protesting. Protest can be costly. But, gradually, public consciousness is aroused.

In Santiago such *rélampago* action is held in the underground (Métro). Participants join the train at different points, converge in one of the middle cars, and, as the train pulls out from a station, distribute their material, leaving at the next station and scattering.

Videos are circulated showing police and military violence against civilians.

In the fall of 1986, Don Irish marched with 10,000 Catholic youth from the outskirts of Santiago to the cathedral at Maipa on a walk for life (*peregrinación por la vida*). The director was quite explicit in urging the youth to challenge the Pinochet régime and demand jobs, education and personal security. There were guitars and liberation songs. Virtually everyone carried a small wooden cross, which would be raised simultaneously high in the air. One marcher gave a handful of crosses to an armed soldier, who handled them in a very gingerly manner!

So witness continues, and grows.

Source: Don Irish in *Solidarity*, Dec. 1986.

100 Dethroning Marcos

The dictatorship of General Marcos in the Philippines seemed secure. There were disaffected Muslims, but Marcos ignored them. There was a rebellion of left wingers but his army was containing them. Anyone else was killed, clapped into prison or driven into exile.

The leading exile, and hope of those who were opposed to the régime, was Benigno (Ninoy) Aquino. He took the courageous step of returning to Manila. As he came down the steps of the aircraft he was shot down. No one had much doubt that Marcos was responsible.

The opposition seemed driven into quiescence. In fact there was a seething volcano underneath. Hildegard and Jean Goss-Mayr, both Catholic, both pacifist, she Austrian and he French, perhaps the most noted international advocates of nonviolent methods, went to the Philippines. There they talked with Putz Aquino, the dead man's brother. He told them that there was a massive reaction against the corruption and violence of the Marcos régime, and that he had access to all the armaments he needed for insurrection. But he was reluctant to plunge the country into civil war. Yet he could see no other way.

The Goss-Mayrs showed him that there was another way, one which offered more chance of real success, active nonviolence. Violent revolution creates an escalation of violence, polarizes the divisions, making reconciliation more difficult, forces the revolutionary party into a military hierarchy, so that even if it is successful, it only replaces one power group by another and does not transform the system, often creating a new power struggle within the revolutionary party. Nonviolence is essentially free from all these defects. At least it was worth giving it a chance. But it requires every bit as much training and discipline as military action.

Putz Aquino agreed and the Goss-Mayrs embarked on a series of training schools in nonviolence: these were later taken up by Richard Deats of the American Fellowship of Reconciliation.

The new movement, called AKKAPKA, had this Credo:

We are a people of God.
We believe in justice, democracy and peace
but first and foremost in the absolute value of human beings
and the solidarity of all peoples.

We oppose all forms of injustice and oppression
prevailing at present in our society,
authoritarian forms of government, discrimination against the poor,
grave violations of human rights, foreign control
of our economic system, our politics and our culture.

We commit ourselves to the upbuilding and maintenance
of a just Philippine society,
but in everything we do we promise:
never to kill, never to injure,
to lead our oppressors into truth
and to remain united in the struggle.

That this Credo may become our way of life
is our humble prayer to God:
may He stand by our side with His help.
We also ask all our sisters and brothers
to make us aware where we have not succeeded
in being faithful to this creed.

There are four notable things about that Credo: it stands for social justice in the light of the value of each individual; it is nonviolent; it is religious; it is a personal commitment.

What happened is history. Under the disciplined commitment and training the revolution which ousted Marcos was very largely nonviolent. When his guard expected to be confronted by a violent crowd hurling rocks and Molotov cocktails they were faced with nuns distributing flowers. They were disconcerted and paralysed. The wave of protest would not ebb. The dictator was ousted, and Cory Aquino, Ninoy's widow, became President by the will of the people. A new constitution was established with the support of 87% of the people. It is concerned with education, human rights, land reform, workers' rights, minorities, nuclear-free territory, the rejection of war as an instrument of national policy, civilian service as an alternative to military service.

Of course, there were other factors behind the success of the revolution. Marcos had overreached himself. He had lost the confidence of the army, and of his US supporters on which he depended. He is a classic example of Tolstoy's theory of history. Napoleon was not defeated by Kutusov; he defeated himself, as, in Tolstoy's view, evil always will. But violent uprising had failed to bring him down, and had Putz Aquino acceded to violence there would certainly have been a great deal of destruction and loss of life, and military support might well have hardened behind the status quo.

Cory Aquino faced enormous problems: the conflict with the Muslims; incomplete decolonization involving economic and military dependence on the US; the rural and urban poor; reactionary elements in the Church; the legacy of corruption; foreign debts, the flight of capital, a prostrate economy, militarism, terrorism and crime. Ninoy Aquino said once that Marcos's successor as President would face the hardest task in Philippine history. He little thought that it would be his widow.

She has been faced with the intransigence of the left-wing guerrillas, and a strong desire from the army to find a military solution: with the unwillingness of the rich to sacrifice their privileges, and the consequently slow progress of agrarian reform; her own peaceable temperament, which prefers to act by consensus rather than autocratic action, which again means a slower tempo; and with the absence of experienced senior people to support her. But however things turn out, nothing can take away from the peaceable revolution.

Source: Personal knowledge.